AF487978

Messages from Ramadear

A collective hope for humanity

By

Kristi Pederson

Graphics and layout by Roxanne Wach
Original cover photos by Marina Gray

ISBN: 979-8-218-13526-3

Introduction

Messages from Ramadear began in a most unusual way. I have journaled for over 20 years which is now more than a habit – it is a way of life. It is a way to vent my concerns and frustrations. But more importantly, it is a way to connect to my spirit guides for clarification and inspiration. I connect to my guides every day in meditation but sometimes mixing it up a bit with writing allows for a different level of communication.

Because I was someone who journaled and communicated with my spirit guides in this way, I thought it appropriate to teach a class on automatic writing. A couple of nights before this online class was to begin, I got the message from my guides that I needed to practice automatic writing if I were to teach the class effectively. At the time I wasn't clear that journaling with my guides would be very different from automatic writing.

Since I almost always listen to guides (and regret it when I don't) I put pen to paper and asked spirit to come through in automatic writing. I expected one of my well-known guides to come through as they always do during a journaling session. Well, the surprise was on me! The minute my pen hit the paper a spirit named Ramadear started dictating to me. Half of me was shocked and the other half just decided to go with it and see what would happen.

Not much happened as I didn't have much time to give that day. I just wrote a couple of small pages without paying much attention to what was coming through and then went on with life. I stupidly forgot about Ramadear and went on to teach the class a few nights later.

About a year later, I was on vacation with a friend and was on the beach with my journal, as usual. Suddenly I got the message to put down my pen and close my journal. I was to enjoy my friend and enjoy the vacation and was to pick up my journal when I returned home, and downloads would begin.

I bit forlorn, I put my journal away. I love to journal and was a tiny bit upset that my guides didn't want me to journal during my vacation as that's one of my favorite and most powerful ways to connect with them. What was up with that!?

The day I returned from vacation, I picked up a pen and my journal and BAM! Downloads began and didn't stop. Ramadear was the name of the spirit coming through to me and reminded me that he made contact with me a year earlier. He was not one of my spirit guides, but was guide to our planet. What?! I didn't even know our planet had spirit guides, too.

Thus began an amazing relationship with this beautiful, funny, and prophetic spirit. He told me how I was one of many chosen to communicate very esoteric things about Earth and humanity, but to do it in such a way that the modern human could understand and relate to. Well now, that's no small undertaking, I must say.

I made a commitment to communicate through spoken and written words to convey messages from Ramadear and the Ramadear collective. What is a collective, you ask? I was told that a collective is a group of spirits communicating from sixth density to various humans; information which is vital to human existence and survival. Earth at this time resides in third density to give you an idea of what sixth density is.

The way this information was to unfold was for me to ask questions of Ramadear. These would be questions I personally have or that I think much of humanity would have. I even went to what I thought was off-track and asked Ramadear some personal questions about me and my work as a psychic medium. I was given that information with the knowledge that most people will want to know the answers to some of these questions, as well as just myself. So, you will find galactic information, planet, and humanity information, as well as personal information intended for me, but hopefully will translate to resonate with many others on their human and spiritual journey.

I wrote this book as instructed by Ramadear and the collective. It was to be written, by date, in the exact way it was channeled through me. So, you might find there is not an even flow as the way most books are written, but hopefully will make sense to those who choose to read it knowing, for once in my life, I did as I was told.

February 4, 2021

R: Hello. May I introduce myself? I am called Ramadear. I hail from the planet Eurates.

K: Are you a guide of mine?

R: No, I am a guide of your planet.

K: Why are you coming through me?

R: You asked, and I am here.

K: Thank you. How do you do that?

R: I work with individuals, like you, to enlighten and inform to keep your planet healthy.

K: Yea well, it doesn't feel very healthy now, does it?

R: No, that is for sure. But it is the personage that is not healthy and therefore affecting the planet. Take care of corruption and the planet will heal itself.

K: True. Thank you. How can I take care of corruption?

R: Be yourself. Teach others. Hold your light. Whenever two or more are gathered there is love. Love is the antithesis of corruption. Practice love in all things you do. Remember, gratitude is also love just in a different package.

K: What else is love?

R: You are. You all are. At the core of humanity is all love. It just gets masked by pain.

K: Now I'd like to talk to my guides. Are any of you ETs?

Spirit Guides: We all are, as are you. But you know that, don't you?

K: Why do people find the notion of ETs so threatening?

Spirit Guides: Because of what you've been taught. Us against them. Divide and conquer. That's what is happening on a small scale in your country right now too. To make yourselves superior there must be someone more and someone less. There must be an enemy. Backwards, eh?

February 16, 2021

K: Ramadear? Are you here?

R: Yes. What is it you need?

K: Clarification.

R: On what?

K: Why have I been feeling anxious these past few days and weeks?

R: You are correct in your thinking that downloads are happening. It just takes the body a while to adjust. It feels like anxiety, but it is merely shock waves.

K: What do you mean by shock waves?

R: Exactly that. The downloads are coming to you in waves. They can be shocking to the routine of your body. Not your soul, but your body.

K: Thank you. Why are the downloads happening?

R: You are ready to step up.

K: Step up to what?

R: The next phase of your development and expression of who you are.

K: OK, who am I?

R: Funny, isn't that what you teach to others, yet you question it in yourself?

K: True. So, again who am I?

R: You are part of the divine energy that is all/everything.

K: Is that what we call God?

R: In a way, yes. In a way, no.

K: What do you mean when you say in a way yes, and in a way no?

R: You call the energy God but others practicing different religions call the energy by a different name. So, when you say God, it is correct unless you practice a different religion then you are incorrect. So, you see a rose by any other name still smells as sweet or in other words a God by any other name is still the same energy which is divine.

K: Thanks for that clarification. Why am I here on this planet?

R: To evolve, observe, learn, teach and to experience.

K: Sounds like everybody else.

R: It is.

K: Do I have a specific thing I'm supposed to teach?

R: Yes

K: What is it?

R: Patience. Ironic, huh? (laughing)

K: Yea, very funny. What else?

R: Love, non-judgement, that people are on their own path.

K: But I'm already teaching that.

R: Exactly. Could you have done this 15 years ago?

K: No.

R: There you have it. You are now open to receiving the downloads. The world needs you now. Your world is on the brink of crisis. A crisis of existence. A crisis of self. A crisis of survival. You are one among many sent to balance and then reverse this trend.

K: Is that why this is happening to me at an older human age?

R: Yes, people will look up to you because you've not only talked the talk, but you've walked the walk. Be proud of who you are. See? Give others permission to be proud of who they are too. They are doing their part just as you are doing yours, but they are expressing their work in a different way.

K: Got it.

R: Do you?

K: OK, getting it. Trying. Working on it. What is the best way for me to teach others in addition to living my own truth?

R: Be a disciple.

K: Huh?

R: Yes, of Jesus but you will communicate in a different way for those that refuse or push back against the name of Jesus.

K: Will my communication be speaking in front of large groups?

R: Absolutely, in addition to small groups and one on one you will be speaking in large groups. Your message is the same for whomever you have the opportunity to share.

K: Is that part of the downloads?

R: Yes! We are giving you the right words (write words) and the right way to say them or better yet communicate them.

K: Thank you. I accept with joy. I open myself to the awakening of the planet for all our healing and highest good.

R: There you go!

October 10, 2021

K: Ramadear? Are you with me now?

R: Always.

K: Where are you from? You told me earlier it was Eurates but can you be more specific?

R: We have the same home. We come from the same origins.

K: Are you going to help me as well as others raise the vibration of planet Earth?

R: I already have. We've been working together for eons. You're just now getting ready to acknowledge it and work with us on a conscious level.

K: Yes, I am ready. I felt a change coming, but I assumed it was tactile, not esoteric. I prefer esoteric, thank you. I'm excited to acknowledge my new partner in you.

R: You will be shocked when it becomes clear how long we've been together, what we've already done, and what's in store for the future.

K: OK, I'm ready. Bring it on!

October 11, 2021

K: Good Morning!

R: Good Morning to you!

K: Thank you. I was told/guided to make contact with you again after the original contact earlier this year.

R: That is correct.

K: I am open to whatever you have to say to me.

R: Really?!

K: As long as it is for my and the planet's healing and highest good.

R: Ok, we're off then!

K: Is this Ramadear?

R: Yes, among others.

K: What others?

R: We are a collective of souls sent to guide you.

K: Where are you from?

R: You already know that – Eurates.

K: Is that a planet?

R: Of sorts – yes.

K: Is it my pink planet? (From my book, *We Are Not Alone: My Extraterrestrial Contact.*)

R: Yes, my dear one! (And a few others) It is a star system.

K: Are you God?

R: Yes, but aren't you too? Aren't we all?

K: True. Is this the best way for us to communicate?

R: For now, yes. You need to get used to hearing from us even though this way will be slow and cumbersome. Eventually you will be able to communicate in a different way, but this is good for now.

K: Is this a bit like the *Conversation with God* books by Neale Donald Walsch?

R: No. It is exactly like the *Conversation with God* books! Neale will eventually be leaving the planet and we need someone else to continue his work.

K: And that is me?!

R: Don't get ahead of yourself. Yes you, among many others. Actually, the information we share is out there for anyone to grab. You happen to be the one who understands the process. Others will hear and listen but will not take it any further. You are willing to ask questions, as well as write it all down.

K: Yes, I am not only willing, but I also feel the power behind this.

R: Good. Because what we must communicate is powerful. Much of the world is ready.

K: OK, where do we start?

R: Right here. Right now.

K: Are you the reason I've been feeling so weird in my body?

R: Yes, as we mentioned before, it is your body adjusting to a new frequency.

K: Usually, when I get this feeling, it is impending bad news, and it won't go away until the news is delivered. Usually, the death of someone close to me.

R: This is a death of sorts too.

K: How do you mean?

R: It is your death. The death of a way of being for you which will extend to a particular group of people on your planet.

(Several months prior to this communication I was in a hypnosis session and was told and shown that I was a first responder of sorts on other planets. These planets needed to be saved, restored, or evacuated. A team of humans, including myself, have been tasked to be first responders. Each team member was in charge of a

certain part of the planet we were working with. For instance, I am always in charge of underwater life. Another team member oversees plant life, another "human" life, etc.)

K: After I die as a human on this planet, will I continue as a first responder on Earth as well as other planets too as I was shown under hypnosis?

R: Ha! You're funny!

K: I didn't mean to be funny. It is my understanding that I am a first responder of sorts on other planets. I just thought that would now include Earth.

R: This is different. More cerebral – less physical.

K: Good. My current human body is in no shape for first responder, physical work.

R: We know. That's part of the reason we are connecting to you now. You've slowed down a bit – enough to actually listen.

K: Ouch, but isn't that the truth? So, how do we begin?

R: We have begun.

K: I know. What I meant is when does the real prophetic stuff begin?

R: This isn't prophetic enough for you?

K: Yes, sorry. Communicating with you is very prophetic. I was referring to messages from you to help save the planet.

R: In time, in time. We need to get to know each other better first and to get a commitment from you that you'll stick with this.

K: I will. I promise. I will do my best to connect with you every morning. It might be a different time every morning, but I will connect.

R: Good. We are grateful.

K: There might be an occasional morning where I can't connect due to travel.

R: We understand. Buy another journal. This one will fill up fast! Ha!

K: Will you be very clear with me on what I need to do?

R: Yes, Write it all down! That's all you need to do for now.

K: Why does the world seem so divisive these days?

R: As your population grows it allows for more younger souls to experience human life on Earth. As you already know, younger souls aren't as open-minded and peace-loving as older souls. Why do you think we sent you Ainslie Macleod's books? Let us clarify. All souls are old souls. When we refer to younger souls what we mean is souls that are newer to the human experience. It takes many lifetimes to acclimate to human life and the human body.

K: If so many younger souls are coming to planet Earth, how do we stop the divisiveness?

R: We can't. Your planet is a planet of free will. In other words, we cannot interfere, but what we can do is help those who are older souls speed up evolution and raise the vibration of the entire planet. Why do you think the veil is thinning? Why has your life so drastically changed course? You're already helping one on one. Now it's time to take this information to the masses. In non-economic terms, you are here to help the middle class – those people who are beginning to experience things from the other side of the veil. They don't know what to do with that information. Just what *Conversations with God* did in the 90's and beyond, you have the potential to do for others. We will give you the right words in the right way and at the right time. You just have to be willing.

K: I am willing.

R: You already began when you agreed to come out as a psychic medium. We are so proud of you and your book. (*Between Earth and Heaven – a beginner's guide to living a spiritual life.*) It's not only a beginner's guide for others, but also a beginner's guide for you, too! That book was channeled, was it not?

K: Yes, it felt that way. I made a commitment to it, and I will do the same for you.

R: Thank you. We appreciate you.

K: Thank you and I appreciate you, too. Is that all for today?

R: Yes, we made the connection and commitments. Let the fun begin.

October 12, 2021

K: You're more enthusiastic than I am this morning. I know I am committed to writing every day, but is it ok to skip a day now and then?

R: It is up to you. Get enough sleep and it won't be an issue.

K: Thanks for a great session with Astara and Orion.

(*Astara and Orion are sound healers and have companies called Astara Raven and Illuminating Hearts*)

R: That was them, not me.

K: Weren't you there?

R: Of course. I was there, but so were many others.

K: Why am I so blind to my own stuff?

R: You're not. You just think you are. Self-fulfilling prophecy. Why do you think you are disappointed in some of the readings you receive? Some just aren't able to tap in and you can feel it. You know the difference between what's right for you and what is a miss.

K: True.

R: Let's focus on more global and galactic things.

K: Yes, let's.

October 13, 2021

K: What do you need to tell me that is important for me and others to know?

R: Your planet is on the brink of catastrophe and most either don't know it or don't care. This has been going on for generations which is now reaching the pinnacle.

K: I understand that we are all here, on planet Earth, for different reasons but sometimes it feels like people can be drones. That they care only about themselves and are oblivious to what is going on around them. They think everyone else is the enemy unless they think and act in the same way.

R: Yes, that is true to a degree. If things don't change your planet will be destroyed as you know it, but it will come back more beautiful than ever. The shift will not be the planet on its access as you have read about. It will be a shift in dimensions.

K: Ah, ok. Exactly what does that mean?

R: Some will traverse the change others will be unable.

K: What exactly does that mean? Is this change going to happen through natural disasters?

R: A change in dimensions is difficult to explain. The shift for those ascending will be seamless. They will notice the change in the way that the world and its inhabitants are kinder, gentler, and now concerned and aware of the environment around them. The disasters you mentioned are not natural at all. They are what cancer is to the human body. Through drought, flooding, volcanic eruptions, Earthquakes, tornados, tsunamis, and hurricanes – they are cancerous reactions to the energy on your planet.

Those that have not ascended will see Earth much as it exists today, only things becoming more violent and people even more self-centered. It will be a seamless transition for both groups.

K: If we are on the brink of catastrophe what can I do as a lone person?

R: You're doing it, but are expecting different results from what will really happen.

K: So, what are those results?

R: It is still unknown the full extent because you live on a free will planet, but the positive changes will happen by you and others doing our work You will be preparing others for the shift in a more non-obvious way.

K: Was I correct when I realized the vision I saw on the craft *(We Are Not Alone…my extraterrestrial contact)* with that huge fire and people running scared? That I couldn't save my family? That by saving others really meant teaching them to save themselves.

R: Absolutely. It's the same difference between give a man a fish or teaching him to fish. That is what's wrong with many religions. They tell people what to do. They don't empower people.

(I had an extraterrestrial event on a UFO where a teacher showed me how to program and then holographic images of a huge fire)

K: Were you the teacher on the craft that day?

R: Ah ha! My cover is broken! I've been discovered! Ha!

K: Wow. This is what you meant when you said I would know what to do when the time was right.

R: Yes. You thought it would be an Earth ending event. It's not. It is event after event which will either break people and they will choose to leave their bodies, or they will have the strength and coping skills to stay and build a better Earth.

K: Will that happen in my lifetime?

R: Yes, but not as the human you are today. It will happen in another of your human incarnations. This lifetime you are practicing skills that will be magnified on a much larger scale in another lifetime.

K: So, when others see and hear me speaking in front of larger groups, is that this lifetime or a future lifetime?

R: Both.

(Very much like you've done in many other lifetimes leading up to this lifetime.)

But most psychics who are like you focus on this lifetime and they don't even realize that they are tapping into other futures and past lives. The short answer is they are tapping into this lifetime.

K: Thank you. If it's going to be one disaster after another, shouldn't I be on stages now giving people information?

R: You are. But the size of the stage is measured to the degree that you work on those speeches, girl!

K: I will, I promise.

R: The timing is now in your hands.

K: Oh God – that sense of urgency again.

R: But it IS urgent. Start small – you know how to do it. An outline is really all that is necessary. Use the chapters in your most recent book as a starting point, but don't let it fall flat. Give people something to walk away with. Yes, they need to hear your stories, but they need to hear them as a tool to empower themselves.

Be the inspiration. Remember when you exhibited your work as an artist? Even with signs, people would ask, "Is this where the art is?" "Could these coasters be used as coasters?" It's exactly the same thing. Some people won't show up. Some people will be confused even with obvious signs, some people are there to learn and ask questions. Others will march in ready to buy and learn what you are selling/teaching because it resonates with them. They understand the value. That is with anything in life; once they understand the value, they will be on board. Your talks need to appeal to all groups except those that don't show up. That's the group you can't save. Use this writing today as YOUR inspiration on what you want your talks to look and sound like.

K: I will. Thank you.

R: Also, going back to your sales background in a very crude way – People don't give a shit about you. They only give a shit about what you can do for them. What is the benefit for them? That's how people have been trained to think. Use that knowledge to build your talks.

K: I will but it sounds fairly insulting to the human race.

R: Like I stated, this was a very crude way of explaining it to you, but it should make it clear that people who are hearing your messages for the first time really need to be led as to how they will benefit. When they benefit, humankind benefits and the entire planet benefits.

October 14, 2021

K: I loved the message of Angie and I writing a book together. The energy was so strong last night that I had a hard time sleeping. The information was that I would contribute on a galactic scale, and she would contribute on a human scale. I will contribute whatever you think is what the world needs to hear and know.

(An update since writing that last paragraph. Angie and I will be writing separate books, not writing one together. The messages will be similar, but coming from different humans, we are having different experiences.)

R: Yes, because there is much people are ready to hear as they begin to awaken. Remember the Robin Williams film with Robert DeNiro, *Awakening*? That's what this will be like – an awakening and awareness from people who have been asleep much of their lives. That's what needs to happen on your planet right now. People need to wake up for their own survival. They will begin to wake up in different ways. Some will read, some will see, some will hear, and some will just begin to know. The time is right for their souls to recognize why they are here. These messages are global, but America seems to be the most in need. The United States is young as a country and filled with young souls and therefore haven't had millennia of years of programming like other cultures. America is still young enough to change or at least reject the programming that's been delivered to them through ancestral programming.

R: It's like reteaching a young child rather than an older person. The child will be more resilient. In other words, we begin with the low hanging fruit. Still there are Americans who will resist as there are humans across the globe who will resist. They are the young souls in adult bodies. The people who understand the fastest are the old souls in the young bodies.

K: I understand. So what messages are we to deliver?

R: That they are coming to your planet to raise the vibration.

K: Who is "they"?

R: What you are calling aliens and extraterrestrials. They are coming in alien form, but they are also coming looking like the person next door which are now being recognized as Starseeds.

K: So how do we tell these Starseeds what to do and why they are here?

R: You can tell, show, and teach in many ways. The first way is for them to recognize the programming they've received their entire lives. That awareness alone can shift energy. We are not talking conspiracy theories here. Those will be discussed on another day. For today, we are talking about programming from well-meaning people – mainly parents and other family members. Then friends, teachers, classmates, bosses, co-workers, etc. They have their own programming and try to pass it on through the generations with the energy that they believe they are doing what is best for the child. In most cases nothing could be further from the truth. It's so hard to reject because, especially with parents, the programming is delivered with so-called love and concern for their children's health and very existence. When people receive information that way, even if it doesn't feel right, they'll believe and allow it. All they have to do is look around and they'll see the exact same thing going on with people around them – even society as a whole, not just individuals. That's what makes it so difficult to reject. Even though it rubs wrongly against their souls, people agree to programming that hurts them as well as the souls around them. It ripples out and further out until you have a society like you're experiencing today – backwards and upside down. All it takes is a few to see the truth.

K: What is the truth?

R: That everything comes from love. No exceptions. Everything people think, say, and do comes from love. It's as simple as that.

K: Wait. It is my understanding that Earth is a school and a hard one at that. We are here to experience human emotions which can be hate, fear, jealousy, rage, etc.

R: This is true, but those human emotions are being exploited. They do exist as dark exists next to light. By exploring all those negative emotions, it lowers the vibration of your planet. In other words, does exactly the opposite of what now needs to happen. Those negative emotions are all fear based. When people are in fear, they are easier to control or program. So yes, Earth has those emotions as something to launch from or kick against and get them to love. They can be experienced but the goal should be to get them to a place of love. As it exists today the goal is to use and magnify those negative emotions, so people stay afraid and thereby give away their strength to anybody else, especially those in power.

Who's power you ask? Those people who we perceive are better and more knowledgeable than we are – our parents, bosses, teachers, and politicians. The truth is, they want it that way, for them to stay in power, which is why it's worked for generations. It's time for a change. The time is now.

October 15, 2021

R: Let's talk politics today.

K: Oh boy, That's a hot topic!

R: It shouldn't be, but it is in almost every country on your planet. Someone who thinks they know best tries to make decisions for everyone. Very few politicians are actual leaders. They are so wrapped up in their own egos that they end up being very short sighted. People do have the right to protest, except in a dictatorship, but the protests don't really matter all that much.

Change usually happens quietly with one or two people just doing things their own way. Others around them quietly join in. It gets to the point where politicians are forced to make changes in the law. What people forget is that politicians really aren't leaders; they work for the people. They're supposed to put into law what the people want. What's happening is that people have lost sight of what they want, so they look to politicians to make those decisions. When politicians do, people get upset, complain, and protest. People need to be clear in their own lives about what they want so that energy can grow into the energy of a city, state, and country. People think they know what they want but they really don't – especially in the United States. It is such a young country, and its people act like the toddlers they are.

Temper tantrums and looking for the next shiny thing to temporarily distract them.

K: Is that why we have uncontrolled consumerism?

R: Exactly. Very little of what you purchase is needed – it is merely wanted. Think of a child's toybox or their room. With too much stuff that child can't even keep track of what they have, so they live in a mess and just want more. That's what the unawakened in your country is like right now – a messy toddler's room. Clean up your mess! It always begins with you.

There is nothing wrong with having beautiful and lovely things that go beyond necessity, but it's become too much. Your homes are getting bigger and bigger to hold all your stuff and still you build storage units to hold more and more of what your huge houses can't hold. When will you open your eyes to the truth? Some of you decide to downsize so you throw things away or donate. All you've done is move things to a different location – a landfill or someone else's home. Your stuff exists. You can't throw it away. Where is away? There's no such place.

We want you to have all that you need to sustain and thrive in your life but start to be aware of what that truly is – it's not what you think. It will take deep thought and commitment to yourself and your planet to make significant change. As the population of your planet continues to grow more things will be bought, consumed, and thrown away. Start thinking about not only re-cycling but pre-cycling. Buy things or create things that can go back to the Earth. Then you can purchase and consume to your heart's content! People want to buy things that last forever. In theory that is great, but the things should be able to last while they are needed and actively used but then be able to disintegrate and go back to feed your planet – not destroy it. You're getting there but have a long way to go. Persevere, my lovelies.

October 18, 2021

K: Good morning Ramadear. I Googled your name yesterday not expecting anything. I didn't know if your name even existed, but saw that your name means wisdom, seriousness, thought, intent, and intuition. How beautiful is that?

R: That is correct and exactly what we are doing here is serious and our intent is to get people to think about the wisdom of the ages being presented to them. Once the information is presented people can then choose how to react. Many will never receive this information. Be aware of this. And even those who do get the information, many will still reject it. That is ok. This information will be in the hands of those who are ready to receive it. Just as it took generations to hurt people, it can take generations to heal them.

K: How do we help them heal?

R: Begin by healing yourself. Then, by giving them the truth. People will begin to recognize the truth rather than the lies that have been presented to them.

K: What lies?

R: That they need someone in charge. That they are not good enough. That there is something wrong with them. That there is a hierarchy of better and worse, and that they will never reach the top without help. The constant comparison of them to someone or something else.

Your commercial advertising is a good place to start. You have a law about truth in advertising, yet there is nothing truthful about it. Marketers pretend to be truthful about ingredients, but then proceed to list poisons either as healthy or they use a description that no one recognizes. Companies act like they are too busy to investigate, or they reconcile with themselves that what little bit they consume won't hurt you. People actually believe that, yet people are riddled with cancers and other diseases. Researchers are coming up with treatments which are poisonous themselves. No one is coming up with a cure although it is staring you right in the face.

K: What is the cure?

R: Stop poisoning yourselves! Stop adding poisons to the food you eat. Grow food in soil that hasn't been contaminated from things put in the Earth, water, or dropped from the sky. You're doing it to yourselves and then wonder why you're sick.

That is the first way to cure illness. Stop poisoning yourselves. The way humans are structured they need to eat different things to nourish the body. Quit shaming people because they eat meat! Quit shaming vegetarians because they don't. Quit shaming! Some bodies need meat. But they need meat that doesn't come from animals who have been poisoned. If your body craves fish, eat fish that hasn't been poisoned by the waters they swim in. If you prefer fruit and vegetables, eat fruits and vegetables which haven't been poisoned by the treated soil in which they've been grown. You're doing it to yourselves, and you don't even know it.

K: Let's talk about wild caught fish.

R: What exactly does that mean? Not raised in fish farms? Raised in an ocean that is completely contaminated? You pay more for fish that has been unintentionally poisoned as opposed to intentionally poisoned? Where is the logic in that? See? You trust companies instead of people with your decisions regarding your health because you're too busy at your day job, working for another company. A vicious cycle.

When you consume healthy food, your body, mind, and soul will respond accordingly. I can hear you now: "But I don't have time! It's inconvenient!" What you don't realize is that you can have both. You can have health and convenience if people running these companies cared about people more than they care about profits and shareholder gains. Your world has created a vicious cycle throughout the generations and it's time to go back to the root cause. The root cause is greed. The greed doesn't just come from companies producing your food, it comes from a growing public demanding convenience and speed. Another vicious cycle. When people begin to awaken, as they already are, they will take more control of what they put in their bodies and how they do it. That means taking care of your environment. It starts there. That's not completely true. It begins with people who are healing themselves and who truly want to assist others in their healing. Kristi?

K: Yes?

R: Didn't you make a commitment to heal many years ago?

K: Yes, I did.

R: You know that meant body, mind, and spirit, correct? You're doing a good job, by the way, but you've really only scratched the surface. You prepare almost all your own food, correct?

K: Mostly, yes.

R: You think that is healthier because you know there are no preservatives. You cook it yourself and preserve it yourself. You even grow some of it yourself.

K: Correct.

R: But you have no idea when you go to the grocery store where or how the food has been grown or how it's been prepared and packaged for you.

K: Correct

R: The convenience of picking up a bag of this or that outweighs the time to do your research.

K: Right now, I'm too busy writing this freakin' book!

R: Would you rather stop?

K: No. I'm just getting frustrated with how deep this goes; how prevalent lies are. How do we even begin to fix this?

R: I already told you. Sidestep your government. Go to the grassroots with people who see the bigger picture. Those who do want to make a difference. They have companies that are not publicly held so the pressure for double digit increases isn't as great. The vast financial difference between the CEO and other workers is less.

K: They are working to survive, and yes thrive, but what does thrive really mean? You thrive while everyone else just survives?

R: No. Thrive means that not only you thrive but you're helping everybody else thrive. It is up to "everybody else" to decide whether they actually want to thrive. To elaborate, everyone wants to thrive but how many choose to thrive? There is a huge difference. It's time to not hold down the masses but lift them up until they can pay it forward and lift others in return, or at least those who choose to be lifted by others.

October 19,2021

R: Let's pick up where we left off yesterday.

K: OK. I believe we were talking about how as a race we are poisoning ourselves.

R: True and in more ways than you know. We discussed poison coming from the air, the ground, and your water systems. You've heard the story of the people of Atlantis destroying themselves because of misuse of technology? That's exactly what you are doing now. History repeats itself, eh?

K: What? Are you Canadian? What's with the "eh"?

R: You don't like it? I thought it lightened the mood a bit.

K: Ok, it does. Continue.

R: With the number of new souls on your planet, they take what is good – the light side of things – and bring out the shadow side. When you hear about Earth shifting on its axis? That is already happening. Your planet is out of balance. New souls outweigh the old souls which shifts the vibration of your entire planet which in turn shifts the balance. Unless balance is restored, you will destroy yourselves… just like all ancient civilizations.

K: I really don't want this book to frighten people. Any good news?

R: Well, people can walk around in ignorance and continue to do what they've always done. Is that the good news you want? Or they can awaken to what's really going on, make changes and live a happier and cancer-free life. The choice is yours. It is always yours. I'm here to bring it to light. You're here to do something about it if you choose. You always have the choice.

K: Ok, let me get this straight. Your job is to give me the information. My job is to pass on this information so those with the proper skill set can implement it. Is that correct?

R: Yes, well put.

K: That's a heady responsibility. What do you mean by skill set?

R: People are born in this human life with certain talents. The people with more scientific minds might work with the problems of poisonous chemicals. Those with the talent healing will work with the problems of energy, etc. We're just asking you to get the word out. Then let others pick up the information and run with it.

K: OK, I promised I would, so here we go.

October 20, 2021

K: Can we talk about something more cheerful today?

R: Sure, if you want but you need to know that to find the solutions you must first identify the problems.

K: I know, but I hear bad shit every time I turn on the news or listen to a conversation between anybody, anytime, anywhere. It's hard to maintain a peaceful, cheery attitude when there is a tsunami of bad news, and now I'm hearing it from you, too.

R: The thing is the news that's being delivered is topical. Surface. It only addresses the problem, never the solution. It's like when you cut your finger and you blame the finger instead of the knife that's sticking out of the drawer. It makes no sense. The problem isn't the bloody finger. And no Band-Aid will help as long as the knife is still sticking out of the drawer. Look at the knife – not the finger or the Band-Aid! That is the root cause.

K: Good analogy. Thank you.

R: You're welcome. That's why you're sick of complaining although you do plenty of it yourself. Because it's always the same thing over and over.

People love to point out what's wrong, but rarely do they offer solutions. And many of those that might offer solutions are really just offering Band-Aids. They are not going to the root of the problem. That's how you came to be such a shaming society. There is a certain badge of honor pointing out when something is wrong which makes themselves a victim. Your society loves its victims. Speaking of your news; it's 20 minutes of pointing fingers and creating victims and two minutes of survival and overcoming adversity. Really? It just encourages people to parrot what they hear which is 2% good and 98% garbage. There are a few who have been sent to the planet to listen to the bad, see the bloody finger but also see the knife sticking out of the drawer. They will offer a solution – put the knife back in the drawer!

Here's the kicker – for every person who says, "Good idea. Why didn't I think of that?" There are 1,000 other people who will complain that the knife is too big for the drawer, or the drawer isn't big enough for the knife. Why do your people find joy in complaining? Here's the theory – they don't. There is an epidemic of unhappiness – a lack of joy in your culture. Quit complaining! Listen to or create solutions. Implement them and be happy! It really is simple, yet most are blind to it. You used to love complaining about your neighbor, didn't you?

K: Yes. I hate noise and disrespect.

R: Why didn't you talk to them about it?

K: Because I didn't believe it would make a difference.

R: True, but you could have asked them to respect your peace and quiet.

K: I just kept thinking they would move soon. I feel like maybe I should move, but I don't know where. My lease isn't up for another eight months. There needs to be a change.

R: You can keep moving or you can make peace with what you have.

K: I'd rather make peace than move. Will you help me do that?

R: Of course.

K: Ok, let's get back to the subject at hand. You're right. I complain, too. It seems like that's when everybody steps up – when I complain, they want to hear about it. When things are good, nobody knows what to say. Why is that? It is almost encouraging to complain. People connect emotionally with you; they add their own stories of woe. When there is good news, it feels like congratulations are certainly there, but then the conversation dies. It's like with good news there is nowhere to go. With bad news people get all kinds of riled up and the conversation spins in all kinds of directions.

October 22, 2021

I missed yesterday. Sorry. Actually, I'm not sorry. I was tired. I know I am committed to Monday - Friday but I think that is too much for me. I'm going to have to back off a bit. I need sleep and rest and it feels like I'm not getting enough of either. What works for you?

R: Whatever works for you.

K: I wrote my last two books on Tuesday mornings. I feel like that's not enough for this book.

R: Like we said, whatever works for you. We would just like for you to continue, persevere, and not give up.

K: That much I know. For now, I won't keep to a structured schedule, but I'll contact you at least once a week – probably more.

Can we start talking about solutions instead of problems?

R: Yes, but with every question you have always begins with a problem. The problem needs to be identified first.

K: Ok, fair enough. As far as our environment, specifically our food, where do we go from here?

R: People need to understand that just eating isn't serving the body. Feeling full is the main goal these days. People need a better understanding that we eat for nutrients so our bodies can function in an optimal way. It would be like filling your car with water instead of gas.

The tank is full, but the engine can't run on water. Today the body does get nutrients from food, but in a small way. Enough to function but not enough to thrive. In addition to minimal nutrients, you're getting poisons. This is also a missing link in people's understanding. Even if you eat food full of nutrients, but that food has been grown in tainted soil, watered by poisoned rain, it will counteract the nutrients in the food. For better results, food should be grown in greenhouses and watered with purified water. For permanent results, stop using poisons, pesticides, and other things harmful to your body just so your food looks pretty and appetizing.

It will take about two generations for the soil to regain its natural state. Let your fields rest! They need rest to replenish their own vitamins and minerals to help food grow properly. Farms today are being run by corporations who are responding to demands. Demands from the public for certain foods are found year-round when there should be a growing season and then there are demands from shareholders for more and more profits. When people start growing their own food, whether alone or in a community garden, then and only then will corporate farms respond. As your middle class disappears and more people are starving or poor, this feeds the corporate machine for more and for cheaper food. It is a vicious cycle.

Your people throw away more food than they eat. Food shortage is not the problem – waste is the problem. Healthy food, waste and distribution are the problems. Learn to redistribute. There are a few creative souls now that are coming up with ways to do that. Selling food that doesn't look "pretty" at a reduced rate. Taking food close to expiration dates and donating to shelters and food banks. These are great ways to begin, but still don't go to the source of poisoned food. Starting in the middle is a start and a good one but you still need to go to the source…where the food is grown. What you feed your animals. How your animals are raised. The bottom line for disease in your culture is to go to the beginning – how is the food grown? How are your animals treated and fed? Not everything is a commodity.

October 25, 2021

K: Let's talk about money today.

R: Money or some form of trade for value is necessary in your society, but it is topsy turvy to use a humorous expression.

K: It is indeed upside down. Who determines value?

R: What IS value? Your corporations are huge in determining this. Many don't value human life when they pay pennies to children and adults for their labor. Yet, when the item is sold the price is inflated, sometimes thousands of percentages. Drug companies produce medication for pennies and turn around and sell at incredibly inflated prices. They lie about the huge costs of research and development. Believe me, many times they make back in one year what they've invested in a new medication.

K: Why can some countries offer the same medication from the same company at a vastly different price?

R: Because they can. It's as simple as that. Morals and ethics have everything to do with it. Greed and profits are always the bottom line. Let's talk about football. You pay your players with multimillion dollar contracts under the guise that their careers are short-lived and that they are at high risk for injuries. What about miners who can barely support themselves? What about loggers? What about people who work construction on your highways and interstates? Are they not worth multimillion dollar contracts since their risk is as much or even more than your sports celebrities?

K: Why is this?

R: Because the people owning the teams as well as the players demand it. The people supporting the teams happily pay for it. What is interesting is that those same people drive on your country's roads and complain constantly about the shape they're in and refuse to pass bills to have them maintained. Why is that? A bridge collapses and people die. Everyone is in shock and disgust, yet they refuse to pay for repairs and maintenance. Interesting, isn't it? People will pay top dollar for football tickets and concert tickets but won't pay a living wage to others to maintain the infrastructure of your roads and bridges. People don't trust the government for good reasons, but they trust corporations. Why is that? There is secrecy in both. There is subversion in both. It all boils down to money – your tool of exchange - it is out of balance and run by people who want to line their own pockets. The public is so busy trying to survive that they don't take the time to research and go down the rabbit hole that has been purposefully created to mislead what is really going on.

K: Pardon me for interrupting the flow but I thought this book was to inspire people. So far, all we've talked about is corruption and greed. I'm not sure I can continue if this is all we're going to talk about.

R: See? You're doing it too. You'll only go so far down the rabbit hole before you tire and want out.

K: It's exhausting!

R: That's what "they're" hoping for! If your mission on this planet is to teach people to stand in their own power, you need to teach them that it can begin with knowledge of what they're up against.

K: Can't I just teach them how to be themselves? Not fall for society's bullshit?

R: Yes, you can do that but you're selling yourself and others short. Fighting a lost battle, so to speak.

K: I have to get ready for an appointment now. Can we pick this up tomorrow?

R: Certainly.

October 27, 2021

R: Are you ready to go back down the rabbit hole?

K: Not really, but ok, let's go.

R: People have been fed lies for so long that they don't know what to believe so many have given up and settled for a "me" attitude. Don't get me wrong. There are many highly evolved people on your planet. But there are just as many and more who can only see five feet in front of themselves. Think about it. When individuals want to do something altruistic, they might donate to a natural disaster or an individual's plight and then find out later, they've been scammed. They lose hope in humanity and end up only believing in themselves and their closest friends who think much like they do. Their world narrows and who can blame them, really? There are younger souls at the bottom of your economic scale, as well as younger souls at the top of your economic scale. Both are young souls fighting against each other. Now on the other hand – there are older souls at the bottom of the economic scale, as there are at the top of the economic scale. How do you tell the difference?

K: Is it important to know the difference?

R: Very

K: How so? Why is it important and how do we tell the young souls from old souls?

R: Trust your intuition. The first level of standing in your own power is to learn to trust yourself. The thing is the younger souls are in need of your love and compassion even more than the older souls. This is where you have it backwards. You tend to shun and punish the younger souls for being young. Would you punish a kindergartner for not knowing calculus? Of course not. You would be kind, loving, supporting, and compassionate towards their perceived mistakes when all they are really doing is learning.

Use your own intuition, your inner GPS to home in on whether it's a young soul who needs your compassion or an old soul who needs your compassion. See? Every living soul needs love, compassion, and understanding regardless of age. No exceptions. Isn't that what you want?

K: Yes.

October 31, 2021

K: Good Morning! This seems to work better for me – to space things out a bit.

R: Whatever works!

K: Why is it exhausting for me to channel you?

R: Because we vibrate at very different rates. Your body has trouble keeping up.

K: What can I do to make it easier on my body?

R: Take care of yourself and keep practicing, writing, connecting. Your body will acclimate. Why do you think a year has passed since our last contact? You had vertigo and head vibrations. That was your body preparing for what you're doing now with us.

K: OK. Got it. I knew downloads were happening, but I wasn't sure what the result would be.

R: Now you know!

K: I'm certainly not crazy about the vertigo, however. Is there a way to raise my vibration without it?

R: We can do it more slowly but that will affect your exhaustion and keep that going longer.

K: Yay. I see the compromise here. OK. Keep going, just make sure I don't fall and hurt myself, ok?

R: We're always protecting you.

K: I really like being full of energy when I do my readings and really appreciate you raising my vibrations to assist with that.

R: As always and so it is.

K: Thank you for a great book signing yesterday by the way.

R: That was you and your guides, not us – not the collective.

K: How are you different?

R: Your guides are assigned to you and you alone. The collective is assigned to your planet. You are just one of the people we work with to get the message out. We all have the same message we just have a different way of delivering it.

K: And what is that message?

R: Love – you really are truly one. Start with loving yourself, truly, madly, deeply. Only then can you love humanity. This can happen overnight, but many of you are so programmed to resist or to fight back that it will take generations for you to really figure it out.

K: Do we have generations? Do we have that kind of time?

R: That is up to you, my dear. See? Even you are resisting. We used the word love to answer your question and you switched it. That, my love, is resistance. To a lesser degree but resistance, nonetheless.

K: You're correct, of course.

R: Always because we do come from love which makes us always correct. When you learn to come from love you will always be correct too. Here's the thing; you will always be correct but that will no longer matter to you because when you come from love nothing else matters – ever.

K: I'm working on that.

R: Everyone on your planet is working on that or they wouldn't be on your planet. Some just work on it in a different way than you. That's what humanity finds difficult. They want people to work on coming from love but in their way – no one else's way. We find that funny. There is only one way to love and that is just to love. But you see, you are here on Earth to learn that. In spirit form, you are all love – there is nothing else. In human form, you learn the opposite. You learn about hate, greed jealousy, etc. You learn what that is as a human, so you understand and appreciate love. Just like you said yesterday – you can't appreciate light without darkness. The best way for you to evolve is to experience what love is not. The only way to do that is to be in human form.

If you choose love, you are never wrong. Isn't that what you came to Earth to experience? We will say that your soul came to Earth to evolve and eventually attain enlightenment. We hope in the end you will all choose love, but we do understand that choosing fear is part of the journey, too. So, you see, you choose – always. But if your choice is layered with judgement of any kind towards another then you really are still choosing fear no matter which side of theory you stand. You see even if you are on the non-believing side of any particular theory you still judge the believing side. You are choosing fear just as strongly. When you choose love, there are no sides. Hero/victim, us against them no longer exists. If we are all one, it would be like you saying your left foot is wrong and your right foot is indeed right. You need both. Both are part of the whole. Both working together make the whole-body function more smoothly. If one foot is working against the other foot, the whole body suffers. It's that simple.

K: Ok, thank you!

November 2, 2021

K: A new day, a new month. What does November have in store for us?

R: More of the same. Change doesn't happen overnight. As you teach – baby steps. That's why it's taken generations for corruption to take over and lead the way. It takes small shifts and changes where people don't even notice or it's so small, they don't say anything. In just a few generations people look back and wonder what happened. The same can happen in reverse. Baby steps to love. If everyone does this in a few generations people can look back at the hurt, pain, and barbaric treatment and be grateful for what they have now. This is happening today, but you're focusing on the negative. Take a minute to look back in your field of study, psychics, mediums, and healers of all kinds were killed and/or tortured. Today, more and more people are embracing what you do.

To balance that, the younger souls are heckling, making fun of things like anything paranormal that they don't understand. When a younger soul doesn't understand something many times they revert to fear. Still, your people are no longer being killed for doing your type of work. Younger souls are not evil – they are just young. They too will gravitate to love given a chance. We all gravitate to love given the chance. Some people are nurtured in a way that makes the path to love a little easier – a little clearer. Others have more challenging beginnings where their path to love is a bit murky. Still, everyone is here to walk the path to love. They just need to be shown how. Some/many people are not given that chance because they are being raised by people who don't know what love looks like, where the path begins or how to trust they're doing it right. Ancestral pain continues until one person stands up and finds a different way. When one person begins to walk the path of love, they can heal generations both behind them and ahead of them. That's how powerful love is.

A fun analogy is to pin the tail on the donkey. What fun is the game if you don't have a blindfold on? You see the donkey, you're holding the tail, you walk up and attach the tail. What fun is that? When you have your blindfold on and someone spins you around – now it's up to you to find your way. But you still have a crowd of onlookers cheering you on and telling you whether you're hot, warm, or cold. When you listen, you get there faster. It's very much like life. We come into human form with a blindfold on. We know our goal, but have been spun around by forgetting who we are in spirit as well as the way we were raised, and therefore have lost our way – the path to love is not clear. We have spirit guides, angels, and loved ones cheering us on. When we choose to listen, we can get there sooner and easier. If we don't listen it is much more difficult to find the path. When we listen to our guides and angels, they will clearly tell us when we are cold, warm, or hot.

K: Ok, that was amazing! Thank you for that perfect analogy. I'm trying to listen. Sometimes it's clear that I am warm or even hot. Many days, however, I am cold and need help.

R: That is just like everybody else, dear one. You are no different. What you do, however, is to guide others as you learn. You don't wait for the degree or certification or whatever is deemed needed to make you an authority. You're not waiting for that because you know that in life all of you have a long way to go but the more of you who are willing to step up, take another by the hand and the lead the way and learn together, the sooner your society can turn itself around and walk the path to love. Blessings to you all.

K: And to you.

November 3, 2021

K: Yes, I feel you want me to write today. Here I am. What is so urgent?

R: All of it is urgent! The time it takes to slowly give you the information and for you to write it down can be tedious. Then to type it, edit, and publish will take another several months. This information is time critical.

K: Yes, I know it is time critical, but I need time off too. I work a full-time job as a psychic medium. As happy as I am to get this information, I still need time to rest.

R: We understand. Rest if you must but, please understand what we're trying to do too.

K: Is there a better or different way to get the information down on paper?

R: You could channel out loud while someone else types.

K: Would it work if I typed?

R: Yes, that would be sufficient too.

K: Ok, I'll try typing tomorrow and see where we get.

R: Thank you

K: What are we going to talk about today?

R: What do you want to talk about?

K: All this urgency and you don't even have a topic?!

R: We have many topics but want to see what's important to you.

K: It's all important to me.

R: Fair enough.

K: At this point, I don't know what I don't know. I need your help in deciding what to talk about and how all the topics are connected.

R: Everything is connected – in all ways. Always – in all ways.

K: I tell people that God wants to experience everything that ever been or ever will be which is why we split off as individuals and come to human form.

R: You are partially correct. God already is everything that has ever been or ever will be. Yes, you are correct in saying that in human form we are here to express that it already exists, but has not been expressed. Do you see the difference?

K: Yes, thank you. In human terms it might be that I have all the clothes I need hanging in the closet but when I'm actually wearing them, I am expressing myself differently. Is that anywhere near, correct?

R: You make us laugh! You are correct in a very simplistic and understated way. We understand that it is difficult for the human brain to grasp much of what we're trying to communicate so any way to simplify it is appreciated. You just do it in a funny way.

K: Well, that's me!

R: Yes, that's you expressing yourself as a piece of divinity which you are – as is every other soul.

K: Does that include ETs?

R: We also laugh at your word ET or rather an abbreviation of the word extraterrestrial. There are countless souls or energy forms which exist. Humans tend to think in a very limited way. Those souls or energy beings can be seen, thought of, or imagined as cats, dogs, snakes, rabbits, trees, grass, rocks, fish, birds. Everything is an expression of God or source. How could it not be? And what we just listed is planet Earth alone! There are billions of planets in existence, many with varied and multiple life forms. They ask the same questions you are asking.

Think of all the third-grade classrooms across every city, state, country on planet Earth. They are being taught many of the same things, but they don't yet realize that. That is also true on a galactic scale. Souls on many planets are being taught the same thing they just don't yet know the "others" exist.

K: Whoa, that's a little mind bending. But put in a way to help me understand. Thank you.

R: Do you really think Earth is the only planet experiencing pain? Not even close. Many, many planets are struggling. Earth is unique in its struggles as is every other planet's struggles. We are here to work with souls on planet Earth as well as other planets to educate so the inhabitants can save themselves. They don't need us. You are doing that on a minute scale right now by teaching people how to stand in their own power. It's a beginning. A small start. Some people will misinterpret and see the word power as dominance. This can be part of the learning process. Start by adding to your talks that standing in your own power is peaceful, confident, compassionate, and above all, loving.

K: Thank you. That is a very good point. I will do that.

R: How many times did you have to repeat anything before it became part of your being? That is how humans learn – by repetition. For good or for bad. Trust what you teach is working. People will learn at their own pace.

November 5, 2021

R: We know you're reading a book called, *The Spontaneous Healing of Belief.*

K: Yes, I am.

R: Interesting perspective and certainly on the right path. Not quite there, but we have hope for the author and for who chooses to read his book.

K: Why do you say that? That comes across as a bit offensive.

R: We don't mean to offend. That is part of what needs healing in your society; a propensity to take offense at almost anything. A defensive attitude slows down progress.

K: How does it slow progress?

R: There you go! Please ask questions rather than planting your feet firmly in a place where you really don't know or aren't sure. Until you have crossed over, and by you we mean any human. You really don't understand the structure of life. The wheres and whys of it all. That's what we love to watch – you trying to figure it all out. It encourages us and gives us hope for the education of humankind.

K: So, what does Gregg Braden have wrong in his book?

R: Now that would be cheating, eh? He is on the right path. He's got plenty right but there is much more to the story of life. He has much of it correct. There is just much more to be uncovered or discovered. It will come in time. The truth will come through him as well as others as the story reveals itself and becomes clearer. Going back to pinning the tail on the donkey, with the veil thinning between worlds, it's as if instead of a true blindfold, you are being given a blindfold that allows you to see shadows. It will help you in your quest. We find it interesting that you've never asked why the veil is thinning.

K: You're correct of course. I've never asked and yet it continues to happen.

R: As society invents ways to be more physically comfortable, they are no longer in a constant state of survival. This gives time for contemplation. You see, the answers are all right in front of you. You just need to take the time to reach out, grab the answers, ask more questions for clarity, and then deliver the messages in a way others want to hear or are ready to hear. It is up to those people who are curious enough to listen to the universe. The universe will reveal all its secrets to those who really want to know the answers and can comprehend what they are discovering. You see, everything really does exist. Many people believe this as true, yet they don't know how to bring it into existence.

That is the next step in your evolution. Bringing whatever you want into existence. Here's the thing; so many of you young souls are waiting for others to manifest so they can use the new ideas for fear instead of love. For every invention, idea, or concept there is a young soul using the information for the negative. It is a constant battle between love and fear. Persevere with love. There will always be light and dark while in human form. Light and dark - love and fear. It is always your choice. Do not be dismayed with the darkness of fear. It will always be there. Follow your heart and it will always lead back to love. We love it when you tell people the goal is that everything you think, say, and do comes from love. That is an evolved soul. It really makes it clear how far people have come, yet how far they still have to go. It did that for you, didn't it? And you're one of the many who are teaching it! Now do you have a perspective where people are at who are NOT teaching it?

We do need to clarify that there are many people living it who do not feel the need to teach it. They teach through living it. They lead by example. Most of these people don't even know that's what they are doing. They just do it because it feels right for them, and they know no other way. They are the ones who really understand. They don't need to be taught because they already ARE what you and the others are trying to teach. You, however, teach as you learn, which is fantastic, but don't discount those people who are not your students. Many understand life on a level you are still learning. They don't learn – they do. The teachers need to learn from them, not the other way around. You want to know what it's like to live from love? Go out on your streets. Your non-profits, your homes, your schools, there are many who already live, think, and talk from love. They are just sprinkled amongst others who live from fear, judgement, and shame, so do not doubt it – they are certainly there.

November 8, 2021

K: Good morning Ramadear.

R: And a good morning to you too, Kristi dear.

K: Ah! Clever. I wouldn't have thought to do that. Thank you, that made me smile this morning and beginning my day with a smile is quite lovely.

R: You're welcome. Are you ready to write?

K: I am. Let's get started. What are we going to talk about today?

R: Love. We're going to talk about love.

K: OK. What about love?

R: People talk about different kinds of love, don't they?

K: Yes.

R: There is love for your spouse, love for your children, love for your family. Love to your friends. Love of life. Love of food. People claim a certain kind of love and are usually quite descriptive or verbal about what kind of love they're expressing or feeling because they don't want others to be confused.

One expression which makes us laugh comes from your LGBTQ community. "I love them, but not like that." Quite humorous because it does get the point across. What they really mean is I care about that person, but don't want to have sex with that person. And as you know, sex is very different from love. You can love a vase but certainly don't want to have sex with it – hmmm maybe some of you do. (laugher) We also hear about unconditional love. Particularly a mother's love for her children is supposedly unconditional love. So, what's the difference between all of these loves? Nothing. Love is love. As humans you don't have the vocabulary to further differentiate or define what you are feeling. Let's go back to the vase. You say you love it, but let's dig deeper. Dig deeper than love, you ask? Isn't love as deep as you get? Not necessarily. We are here on Earth for our souls to evolve. What does that mean again? Everything you think, say, and do comes from love. So, when you love that vase, do you really? Or do you admire it? Or do you wish you had the skill to make it? Or perhaps want to just add it to your collection? Are any of those things love? Well, yes. They all are. Because love is really all that there is. Forever and always. As a human, you put degrees on love. It is still love whether it comes to you in degrees or not. Kristi dear, you have stated many times that you don't believe unconditional love exists on planet Earth.

K: True.

R: Well, you are right, and you are wrong. Unconditional love certainly does exist, but as humans you claim it in degrees and therefore it doesn't appear unconditional.

Let's compare it to the condition of pregnancy on your planet. A person could be 1 minute pregnant and still be pregnant. They don't even know it yet, but it's there. Usually, they claim it once tests prove it. Others will claim it when they get past the three-month marker. Others when it begins to show on the woman's body. Which is correct? They all are. The woman is pregnant from the moment of conception but there are still degrees – unknown pregnancy, 1st trimester, 2nd trimester, etc. But it all leads back to pregnancy, but further along in the process of giving birth, which is the ultimate goal or end process.

The same is true of love. You are all so very loved whether you know it or even claim it. Or even believe it. Yet, you are loved. The more you choose to believe or recognize that you are loved the further along you are until you have the unshakable knowing that you are unquestionably, undoubtably, remarkably loved by your team of spirits, guides, loved ones, council of elders, angels and more. That is like giving birth. To know beyond a shadow of a doubt you are so loved for the courage it takes to be human and forget what love feels like, even if temporarily. Because what your soul knows is all encompassing love. While in human form you experience degrees of love. Unconditional love is still there but as a human you choose to forget that and to experience degrees of love. But love is love – in degrees or all encompassing. You are all learning what it's like to feel love, get love, and lose love. That's part of the emotional rollercoaster you call love. It's the rollercoaster of being human. Love is always there – it never left you and never will. You chose to forget, albeit temporarily. But love is always with you whether you know it, claim it, show it, or even give birth to it. It is there forever and always.

K: Wow! That was pretty impressive and succinctly put thank you.

R: We thought so. Did you "love" today's message?

K: Actually, yes, I did "love" it. I can't wait until I'm able to share your messages with whomever wants to listen. Hopefully, they will love it as much as I. Until tomorrow.

November 10, 2021

K: It's been a month since we've been sharing information. I know it began a year ago but in earnest, just a month ago. It feels like we've been communicating forever.

R: We have. But you just now began writing it down.

K: If we've been communicating forever, why haven't I felt you before last year?

R: You have felt me. You know me, too. It just wasn't time to share the information until now.

K: Why now? And how do I know you other than now in this way?

R: You are ready, the planet is ready. Humanity is ready.

K: Ready for what?

R: To save themselves.

K: To save themselves from what?

R: Themselves. Humanity is just now awakening to the fact and idea that you really do create your reality. They've just chosen to create a reality of pain, suffering, and imbalance. It's just as easy to create a reality of love and abundance. It's true that all "men" are created equal. All souls were created at the same time in equal fashion. Some choose to inhabit a vehicle called a body. That body can be human or what you call aliens. Souls choose that vehicle to inhabit knowing full well what they are up against or what they will be learning and experiencing. What they are learning and experiencing is pain, suffering and inequality, at least on planet Earth. On other planets they learn technology. On others science. On others they experience things humans are yet incapable of understanding. Each planet offers a different experience to help the soul evolve. Earth offers emotions, which is one of the most difficult because it sets the stage for inequality. What humanity is just now beginning to realize that you can come to Earth to experience emotions, but you can also choose which emotions. You don't have to choose greed, jealousy, hate, or fear, you can just as easily choose love, support, and sharing.

You have so many new souls on your planet who don't yet have the skills or experience to know they can choose. Many are born to parents who are also young souls and therefore teach their young only what they know. Isn't that how we all learn? By copying or mimicking those who came before?

You and I, as well as countless others, are here to balance the young soul's energy and teach them that they do indeed have a choice and a voice. That is what free will is all about. Think about a kindergarten classroom. There might be 20-25 young five-year-olds but there is one teacher with maybe one helper. Those one or two adults or older people can teach an entire classroom of children. That's what it's like on Earth; older souls or Starseeds are planted in different parts of your planet, in different countries, in different cities, even in different neighborhoods to affect change. But not everyone needs to change or wants to change. But you do need enough people to change to balance the energy of your home – Earth. Today's younger souls far outweigh older souls but just like that kindergarten class, it most of the time takes only one to teach love and acceptance to affect change in a group of people. You can feel the change can you not? As the veil thins, what it really means is that enough older souls and Starseeds are now present to lead the way. Younger souls are beginning to awaken or beginning to learn which makes the veil appear to be thinning. It really isn't. It appears to be thinning, but it is actually just young souls beginning to learn – beginning to comprehend life beyond themselves.

November 12, 2021

K: I hope it's appropriate. I want to ask about me instead of something to do with the planet.

R: Yes, go on.

K: I feel like my readings haven't been as strong as usual. Is that true? If so, why? And what can I do to feel like readings are strong again?

R: It's perfectly acceptable to ask personal questions. You are part of the whole, which means anything affecting you also affects others, the planet, the galaxy, the whole.

K: Thank you.

R: Your readings are actually just as strong if not stronger. It doesn't feel that way mostly because you don't remember readings. You're actually tuning in to a deeper level which makes memory almost impossible. You are the vehicle for delivering the words of spirit. They are not your words. It feels like it many times because, as the vehicle, you use your expressions, gestures, and emotions. An example is when you were reading for your friend earlier this week, you felt that the words were not poignant, specific, or shocking like you, Kristi, wanted them to be, correct?

K: Yes, correct.

R: What happened later?

K: She told me the words were verbatim of what she and her boyfriend discussed earlier in the day.

R: See? Your ego was trying to get in the way by wanting to impress your friend. You were fighting spirit's words which are always perfect. Keep check on your ego! Let spirit do their job! Trust! Maybe you should use some of your own oils! Ha!

K: Very funny because it's true. Sadly. Damn ego.

R: Don't discount your ego. You need your ego to humanly separate yourself from others. Just be aware that it can interfere with you doing your job – your work. Ego is what makes each person different. If we all come from source, how are you all different from each other? It's ego! You just need to keep your ego in check. An unhealthy ego is not what the world needs right now. When you have an understanding that your ego makes you different but not better or worse than anybody else you are on the right track.

K: I keep working on that. Thank you.

R: Now back to your readings; they are strong. They are filled with guidance. Trust yourself, trust spirit, trust the process.

K: OK, I will. I will continue to be more aware and try.

R: That's all we ask.

K: I can see how this could be a message for humanity. Trust – yourself mostly. But don't let ego get in the way no matter what your work might be.

R: Exactly. Well said. Ego is strictly a human experience. Older souls are starting to understand this. You need your ego to temporarily separate yourself from source, but you are still source. Feeling separate from source can feel lonely or even off putting.

In an attempt to feel good, you self-medicate – the ego becomes inflated and only exacerbates the feelings of alone or loneliness. This is particularly true of younger souls. They miss "mom and dad" (source), so they act out, throw temper tantrums in a way to get attention or get their needs met. Older souls miss source too, but they know "mom and dad" will be back and they will once again be part of the whole – or even more succinctly, know that they always were and always will be part of source. There is no separation. It is an illusion. It's like being part of a family. Whether mom and dad are at home or are gone for the evening, you are still a family. The family doesn't become whole only when mom and dad return. You are always a part of a family whether you choose to be or not – whether you leave home or not – whether you discontinue communication with your family or not. You are still part of that family. The exact same thing can be said of your relationship with source. You are source – you are an individual expression of source whether you acknowledge it or not. Even older souls discontinue their relationship with source to experience what that feels like. That is not so much ego-based in older souls as the opportunity to learn and experience another level of the soul evolution.

November 14, 2021

K: While journaling this morning I was guided to ask you a few questions.

R: Yes, continue.

K: Who are you?

R: I am Ramadear, as you well know. I am the voice for you from a collective of souls assigned to help your planet.

K: What can you tell me about your past?

R: There is no past. There is only now.

K: OK, I get that but, what I'm asking is where do you come from and why you?

R: I – we – come from source just as you do. Why us? Our question goes right back to you as why you Kristi dear? We all have jobs to do. Think of it in Earthly terms – say the running of a retail store. Some souls are on the floor helping customers, some souls are the customers. Some souls manage the employees, some souls decorate the store. Some souls buy the merchandise for the store. Some souls clean the store. Some souls pay the bills, some souls count the money as it comes in. Do you understand? It takes many souls with different skill sets and talents to run that business properly. All have a job to do. The same is with you and me (us) The "store" is Earth. Every soul living on Earth has a job to do. Although I (we) am not living on Earth we have been assigned to help Earth run smoothly. You have the same assignment only from a different location – a different vantage point if you will. But we have the same mission to help the Earth run smoothly.

K: If that is so, why is the Earth in such disarray? Why, as you state, are we on the brink of a crisis?

R: Let's do the store analogy again. When you have too many customers wanting something there is not enough supply to meet the demand. Customers throw their trash away but there is no employee to collect said trash or no place to put the trash because bins are full. There is not enough merchandise to satisfy customers' demands. There are fewer and fewer stores so more and more people go to the only stores that are left. The same is true of Earth. People throw their trash until now, there is nowhere else to put it. People are buying electricity, fuel, and always asking for and demanding more until the Earth has no "merchandise" or anything else left to sell. There is no longer a balance between customer demand and merchandise to be sold or employees to manage the running of the store. Many owners or presidents of each "store" (country) on your planet are corrupt. They just want to get paid and don't really care about the store (country) or its employees (citizens). You and I, among many, many others, are trying to educate, enlighten, and help restore balance to your stores (countries) and therefore your planet. It's like a crisis management group being hired to save a store from bankruptcy. I believe it's called chapter 11 reorganization. People were brought in to help restore balance. That's who we are as a collective. We are the crisis management team brought in to restore balance. You are an employee who is here to communicate to customers what needs to be done to restore balance. Does this clarify for you?

K: To a great deal, yes. Thank you.

R: It is our pleasure and our job. We are grateful you are listening.

K: I am. Why is there so much controversy surrounding channelers?

R: Not all channelers are listening properly. Not all customers care if there is balance. They want what they want, and they want it now. Much like a three-year-old, younger souls are unaware of balance. They think of themselves. They are incapable of seeing the bigger picture. Believe it or not, that is part of the balance we've been discussing. It's just like we have too many three-year-olds (younger souls), so balance is off. Older souls are volunteering to come to Earth to see the bigger picture and to help others see the bigger picture to create balance once again. Without balance, those younger souls (three-year-olds) will never get what they want when they want it because it won't exist. In other words, the Earth won't exist so younger souls will no longer have the opportunity to evolve. Do you see? It's an even bigger picture than what you were seeing.

K: Much bigger!

R: You must learn through us so you can communicate with others. Let those three-year-olds have the opportunity to evolve into four-year-olds and eventually older souls. Let's help them, shall we?

K: Yes! I will do my best to listen and then pass on your knowledge to those others who are ready to listen and evolve.

R: For this, we thank you.

November 16, 2021

R: Give us a minute to collaborate.

K: OK. What do you mean by collaborate?

R: To get together on today's topic.

K: OK. What is today's topic?

R: That's what we are discussing.

K: Should I come back later?

R: No, not necessary. We're going back to the subject of hate today – we just decided.

K: Well, now there's a topic!

R: People think the opposite of love is hate and that is not true. The opposite is fear. People claim to hate something when it simply means they feel out of control in some way. They feel powerless. Let's look at some examples: I hate my boss. What they are really saying is I don't get to express myself in my way around my boss. Or I don't feel heard or appreciated or acknowledged by my boss. In other words, their needs are not being met. That is the crux of hate. In some way, needs are not being met.

I hate broccoli – really means my need for the experience of tasting and eating food which tastes delicious to me is not being met.

I hate that sweater. What that really means is I don't like the color or style of that sweater because I don't look or feel good in it. Or my need to look and feel good is not being met.

I hate that person really means that that person is not giving you what you need; love, appreciation, acceptance, acknowledgment, or they are acknowledging you but they're doing it in a way that is negative to you. You all want love. You all want to be heard, appreciated, and acknowledged for who you are and the work you do. Why do you think there is applause at the end of a play or symphony? Or a performance of any kind? People are acknowledging and appreciating the performance. Look at one of your favorite human past-times – football. There might not be applause as a way of showing appreciation but just by showing up to a game is appreciation for what the attendees are expecting the performance to be. A team loses too many games and fewer and fewer people show up to acknowledge a good performance. They might even say they hate that team. What they are really saying is that particular team, players, coach, or even their team colors are in some way not meeting the needs of the watcher. So, you see, hate is not really the opposite of love. It is merely a way of stating your needs are not being met in some way. Next time you hear someone claim that they hate something, ask why. It is doubtful they will come up with an explanation that doesn't include how their needs are not being met. Hate and fear, which are the true opposites of love, are close cousins, however. Let's talk about fear another day, shall we?

K: That sounds good to me, Thank you.

November 16, 2021 (afternoon)

R: Thank you for returning so soon.

K: I kind of had to. You were downloading messages during my walk. I didn't want to miss anything.

R: We are going back to balance which we discussed a few days ago. Balance is imperative in everything. It begins with body, mind, and spirit. If each person were in balance with body, mind, and spirit there would be no need for us to help balance the planet. It would automatically be balanced because each human is balanced. Let's look at the body first. That's what disease is – an imbalance in the body. There is a disconnect between the organs, the bones, the muscles, and the skin, etc. As you already know, all diseases or illnesses begin with emotional imbalance. Let's stick with the body for now. We'll address mind and spirit a bit later.

You can argue, as I know you have, that sometimes disease is a person's life path. That is true but it still begins the same, the origin is the same. A person while planning their next life may set the stage for imbalances in the body. They come into this life with health issues or even develop them later in life. It still stems from the soul creating that imbalance for the life ahead. If disease is not part of the life plan – free will – it is still an imbalance, but the origins may be different. For instance, say somebody was abused emotionally. They can create an unconscious belief system that says they are undeserving. They interpret the abuse they receive from others and internalize it into their body. A beautiful way to handle this is to start before any disease has taken hold. This also works while disease is present but isn't prevention easier? Start with your brain and tell your brain how much it is loved. Then move on to your eyes, your mouth, your ears. Continue to your bones, your muscles, your skin, your hair. Keep going until every organ in your body has been addressed. Just like you, who wants to be loved, your body, "peace by peace," wants to be loved too. Begin there. Instead of counting sheep at night, pay attention to each part of your body and send love to every nook and cranny and see what happens.

Let's move on to your mind. Not your brain – your mind, for there is a distinctive difference. Your brain is merely an organ. An organ which stores information. Your mind is the information. Think of it this way – your brain is a computer, but your mind is the data or software which is loaded into the computer. That data can be deleted if it no longer is relevant to the computer or to the person accessing the data. The same is true of the mind. The data which was programmed through the years may no longer be relevant to the body, brain, or the person who houses it. It can be deleted program by program and then reprogrammed with new data which better serves the body and the individual. Is this easy? Sometimes yes, but most of the time no. When receiving programming from, let's say an abusive parent, it will stay in the brain for as long as that child still has access. We are here to learn, experience, and accomplish things.

When we receive data or programing which derails what we came here to do, it creates an imbalance in the mind. We need to find others who are willing to teach or mentor us how to delete old files in our minds and reprogram our minds with new data which will be conducive to helping us reach our goals, learn our lessons, and accomplish what we came on this planet to do. An imbalance in the mind can snowball and also create imbalance in the body.

So now you ask, what about mental illness? The same holds true as in the body. If it is part of a life plan, it is still the soul setting the stage for the upcoming life. If it is not part of the life plan, there are many things which cause an imbalance of the mind – abuse from others, drugs, alcohol, food, chemicals as well as other things. You must be mindful of what you put in your body because not only does it affect the body, but it can also affect the mind just as much.

Let's talk about spirit next. Your connection to spirit is the third leg of the triangle. All sides of that triangle are equally important. Paying attention to one side more than another will again create imbalance. Connection to spirit is your link to keeping balance in the other two areas.

Your spirit guides, angels, deceased loved ones and your council of elders are there to help you not only keep balance but help you bounce back from learning those hard lessons, keep you on track to learn, accomplish, and experience what you came here for. The highest form of love will keep you in balance with the universe. By staying in balance on all three sides, body, mind, and spirit you will learn, grow, and reprogram yourself to be the person you came here to be. Life isn't easy. It wasn't meant to be, but it can be easier for you than it is now or has been in the past. Connect to spirit. Connect to your guides, angels. Loved ones, and elders. They will guide you and help you stay in balance or get back in balance.

K: Good morning and happy lunar eclipse.

R: And the same for you! Do you want to talk about lunar eclipses this morning?

K: Uh, ok. What is a lunar eclipse?

R: Technically it's when the sun and the moon appear to cross each other. They are always the same distance from each other but appear closer. It's the rotation of the Earth that causes this. The sun and the moon are fixed but the Earth is not. It's during certain cycles that eclipses happen; both lunar and solar.

K: You know, I'm going to have to verify this before I can put that info in a book.

R: Of course, please do. Always educate yourself before you attempt to educate others.

K: I just Googled it and yes, the sun is fixed but the moon orbits around Earth which means it is not fixed.

R: Ah, but it is fixed, it's just not stationary. It is fixed in the way it moves, rotates, and orbits. The sun is stationary. There is a difference.

K: Well, ok then.

R: That's why when they say your partial eclipse is the longest in 580 years. Eclipses happen on a very regular basis. Check your history. What makes them unique to you is that some of them only happen once in your lifetime. But in your lifetime, you will see several lunar and solar eclipses, but many can only be seen in certain places on your planet – again making them rare. So, frequency and location are the factors at play here. Also, the weather. If it's cloudy or raining this may obscure the view as well. The eclipses don't change, they are fixed with the rotation and placement of the Earth and moon. What does change is your technology and people's interest, and your ability to predict the next one and report it to the people. So, these events have been going on for millennia but your ability to see, study, and research, and report is very new which makes it exciting, yes?

K: Yes, it certainly does!

November 21, 2021

K: Thank you for having the explanation of the lunar eclipse be a topic of conversation. During a meeting Friday night, a clearer explanation was given to me in a way I was able to understand. The orbit of our planets is different than what we've been taught. No wonder I was having a hard time understanding! The sun is stationary in the way it is part of the orbiting of our solar system, meaning it doesn't spin. The moon is fixed meaning it too is part of the orbiting of our solar system, but we only see one side of the moon. We never see the "dark" side. All the other planets rotate but still in a specific pattern. So, the orbit looks more like a helix than a bunch of circles.

R: We thank you, too, for your continuing education. When something doesn't feel right to you, please do research until you have a better understanding of what we are trying to communicate with you. This is important for your own understanding as well as the way you communicate this information to others.

K: My next question still has to do with not only the lunar eclipse, but the entire rotation of orbiting planets. Does it or how does it affect human behavior?

R: That is a loaded question. We will try to break it down into words you can comprehend. In many ways, the movement of Earth, other planets, and your entire solar system doesn't affect human behavior. It is what it is. But, in many more ways it has everything to do with human behavior.

K: OK. Tell me how and why.

R: Yours is a planet of free will meaning you have choices and flexibility. When planets are positioned in a certain way however, it affects the energy of your planet and therefore the energy of its inhabitants – meaning humans as well as all life forms. War is probably the best example. When your planet is positioned in a certain way it can be aggravating or upsetting to certain souls. It is another lesson in the Earth school. When things are rocky, do you revert to your primal selves and use violence, or do you use the skills you've acquired through many lifetimes to find a more peaceful resolution?

K: Wow! Crazy!

R: Crazy is correct, although we prefer terminology which is less offensive.

K: Sorry, but still…

R: Think of it in today's human behavior. Two people are in conflict whether in a work situation, family situation, or neighbor situation. At work, do you fire someone? Do you talk about them behind their back? Do you shun or dismiss them? Or do you teach and mentor and include them until they understand what is expected? The choice always begins with you. Your behavior. Then, it is up to the other person to choose how they will react. Will they go into a deep depression for being fired? Will they sue? Will they mow down the entire workplace as payment for what was done to them? Perhaps they will be grateful when inclusion and mentoring is offered, and they will blossom. They might even choose to become or stay the victim as they perceive themselves to be. The choice then becomes theirs. But the first choice is always yours when conflict presents itself. The same is true in any kind of conflict. Whether it be two people in any situation. When the energy is there, it is to set the stage for a lesson. That lesson is the same whether it be between two people or more, two or more countries, or eventually two or more planets. It is part of the design to give you free will options on how you react to energy shifts which are caused by the movement and rotation of your planets. When you really break it down even further, it is always between two people. Even when it appears to be between two countries. It is actually the two leaders of those countries in conflict. They have the power to direct millions of others to act on their behalf making it look like two countries at war, when it really is two individuals. So how are you going to react during the next energy shift? Will you gather the troops to be on your side or will you handle the conflict with grace, courage, peace, and love? The choice is always yours on how to begin. Then, the choice is always up to the other person on how they choose to react. You once overheard someone say you have to fight for peace. Hearing that caught you off guard, didn't it?

K: Yes, it certainly did. I heard it come from a person I assumed was peaceful and awakened.

R: Well, what you don't realize is that person was correct!

K: What?!

R: You do have to fight for peace, but the disconnect happened when he began thinking that the fight was external – involving guns, ammunition, bombs, etc. The real conflict, as always, comes from inside yourself. Always, in all ways. The fight always begins internally. It's when you can't find the peace within that you go external and blame others. Their reaction can be to understand your internal battles or to get defensive and externally fight back. Are you beginning to see that everything begins with you? Always – in all ways.

November 23, 2021

K: I saw a picture earlier today of several human eyes in comparison with the universe. They looked startingly similar. The thought entered my head that is it a possibility that humans are small enough and insignificant enough to maybe be living on the surface or within an eyeball? We think we're all that and a bag of chips when all we possibly are is just a bunch of specs on the surface of a universal eyeball.

R: Your observation is interesting. While in some ways you are correct, you are also incorrect. The ways in which you are correct is in ratio. Humans on planet Earth are as small, actually even smaller, as what you are thinking in relation to Earth and the known universe. In scale, it would be similar to the comparison you mentioned. Where you are wrong is when you mention humans being insignificant.

Let's go back to your eyeball. If one of the specs, colors, or shapes changes it affects the whole. One thing changes and a person could be blind. They could be nearsighted, colorblind, etc. Each piece and part of the eye is what makes an eyeball very significant. Just as important is every person, every living thing on your planet and indeed on every other planet in the universe. Everything that exists is vital to the health and wellness of the universe just as everything you do with your eyes is vital to your eyesight. That's why it is so important to take care of your eyes – so you can "see" properly. Now what is happening to your planet is that people are not taking care of it – so now they are not "seeing" properly. Many do not see that they are destroying their own home. They do not see that everything has consequences. Just like putting garbage in your eyes. You would never do that, yet many do. Staring at the sun for too long will burn and permanently damage your eyes, yet people do that. The same is true of your planet. People create more and more garbage and dump it thinking it won't matter. It matters deeply. People use chemicals in the air and on the ground which are now quickly destroying your shield against sun damage. People know this and yet continue to do it. They harm and destroy their own home which is akin to harming and destroying their own eyesight. In both ways people can no longer see but it is of their own choosing. Some souls are noticing and are vigilantly trying to stop the tsunami of other's actions as well as repair previous damage. It is helping but not enough and not soon enough.

K: So, how do we fix this?

R: In many ways it is like splashing acid in your eyes. There is no repair – the damage is done. However, as in advances in eye surgery, new ways are being developed to restore eyesight. New ways are also being developed to make waste biodegradable. That will help slow down the damage currently happening. Some people embrace change and others will fight it always.

K: Why do people resist saving themselves and their planet?

R: Because they choose not to see. As of now, it's inconvenient for them to change, so they resist. Your policies need to change to create a drastic halt to what's happening. Living on a free will planet makes that more difficult. There is an individual on your planet today who is working on a way to safely destroy waste which already exists. This is revolutionary. It is in the testing phase now. What is trying to be managed now is that this new way to shrink or evaporate existing waste, including plastics, won't create another problem for your planet – short term or long term. This is truly exciting for us to see.

K: When do you think this will become public knowledge?

R: We can't say for sure, but it looks like in the next five years testing will be ramped up. As long as other people or governments don't try to stop it, this has the potential for radical change for your planet's survival.

K: Why would someone stop it, for goodness's sake?!

R: That's what being human is all about. For every new idea there will be someone who finds out what's wrong with it. Now it's to determine which side has more power behind it.

November 25, 2021

K: Let's talk about Jesus today, ok?

R: OK. What do you want to know about Jesus?

K: I want to know who he was and why he was here on Earth and why he has lasting power for people.

R: OK. Let's get started. Jesus was and is a star being who was more powerful after his passing than he ever was in life. Other's writings of him are what has kept him in the forefront. This is all part of the divine plan, however. He came to Earth to teach love, kindness, patience. He did that and more. He was very aware of being a star being. Some of the lost or destroyed writings about him talk about this.

K: Do those writings exist anymore?

R: Some do. They are in the archives associated with the Vatican. Others have been permanently destroyed. Jesus had a great many followers while on Earth but his teachings and written catalogs of those have helped his influence not only last, but magnify as the years progress. As your planet is in crisis now it is more important than ever to follow his teachings. But as you can clearly see, that is not happening. People are pulling away from religion. They think religion and Jesus are one in the same. They are not! Not even close. Through the years religion has morphed into a way for the church to have control over man. God and Jesus have nothing to do with religion. We don't know how to state that more clearly. God and Jesus have nothing to do with religion! Jesus is the son of God to be sure – but so are you and so is everyone you know. God is all. God is source. God is creator. God is everything in every way in all things. Jesus is God in human form just like you and everyone you know and everything you see. That includes your precious pets. It includes your oceans, deserts, mountains, rocks, and trees. They are all manifestations of God. Isn't it magnificent? Jesus is the same. But Jesus came with very special teachings. You, Kristi, like to use the wording "Lead by example." That's what Jesus did. He led by example but taught and showed others what and why he did what he did. That's part of the power of his teachings. He didn't stand at a podium and pontificate; He did the work. That's part of what is lacking in your society. Too many people talking about what others should do while not doing the work themselves. Let's tweak JFK's words a bit, shall we? Ask not what humankind can do for you. Ask what you can do for humankind.

K: Wow, which is beautiful and perfect.

R: Yes, it is.

K: Here is a phrase I've never understood. Jesus died for our sins. Nobody has been able to explain that in a way that makes sense to me.

R: That's because it doesn't make sense. The way many people interpret that is a major guilt trip. Humans put Jesus on a cross and killed him so everyone who has lived since must pay the price for that killing. This is simply not true. Quit buying into that guilt trip. It is a waste of time and energy which could and should be better spent helping others because of the joy of doing it – not because Jesus died for your sins. Continue learning and emulating the life of Jesus for he truly was a prophet. But do it the way he did it – he was there for the people who needed him – just as he is today. Don't do it because someone else said you had to, or you'd go to hell or you're a selfish lout. Do your work out of love. Do everything from love – just like Jesus. Guilt is not only a wasted emotion, but also a harmful emotion. It vibrates at an extremely low level. Raise your vibrations by thinking, speaking, and acting out of love. Watch your world change.

November 28, 2021

K: I think I'd like to talk about fear again today.

R: Sure, ok. Fear is what drives most people. Fear runs their lives, and they don't even know it. Even if you tell people that, they won't believe you. They might admit to being fearful of certain things such as being hit by a car or having a child get hurt, but they will justify their fears. They will lie to themselves and say it's concern or love. They are fooling themselves. It is 100% fear they are acting upon because of how it will affect themselves. Your society, in particular the U.S., is in a critical place, as we've already discussed. This is caused because of fear. All of it is caused by fear. Does that surprise you?

K: Yes, actually it does. I knew fear was running rampant, but I really had no idea that everything is caused by fear.

R: If fear is the opposite of love, and it is, then everything that is not done from a place of love is fear- based. Let's begin with garbage. Real garbage – the stuff you throw away, not the garbage you all carry in your head.

K: How is garbage related to fear?

R: You buy things you don't need. That includes food, toys, clothing – everything. For convenience's sake, these things are plastic or wrapped in plastic – many times, both. The fear of not having enough – enough time to grow your own food, enough time to cook your own food, enough time to even go to the grocery store, enough money to buy things that biodegrade. The fear that you will appear less than if you don't keep up with what your neighbors have. The fear that if you drink tap water, you'll die so you buy water in plastic bottles. It is true that much of your tap water is unsafe to drink, but it is still a constant race against fear to fill your homes and souls with stuff which is nothing but tomorrow's garbage to make way for the next convenient – make your life easier thing. When you throw things away, where is away? You're kidding yourselves. There is no such place as away. You fear you can't afford, can't find things that biodegrade. That fear is exacerbated by the fear that others will shame you and make fun of you if you start paying attention. That only comes from their fear – that if you change then they'll be forced to change too. It is easier to shame and belittle than to change.

With each new creation or invention there is again balance. Someone will see the good this new invention or discovery can bring and someone else sees the other side, the side that comes from fear.

K: What does fear look like?

R: Let's talk microwave ovens. One person sees the convenience. They might think that they are better than because they've got the latest and greatest new thing. There is the fear of being less than showing its face.

Then they buy food wrapped in plastic to put in their microwave. This is the fear of not having enough time or energy to grow or cook their own food. Another person will look at a microwave and see the potential dangers that the microwave will emit radiation or loss of nutrients in food or disrupt hormonal balances. That is fear, too. But on either side of the equation people will justify their opinions and shame the other side without realizing that they are talking from the same side of the coin – fear. In the meantime, your dumps, landfills, and garbage bins are filled with plastics as well as with microwaves that were not made to last. They were made by someone who has a fear of not making enough money to live on if people don't continue to purchase their product. Fear is insidious. It is gradual but deep and unrelenting. Now let's talk about the garbage that resides in your mind.

K: Can we continue this tomorrow?

R: Of course.

November 30, 2021

R: OK, let's continue the discussion of fear and garbage in your mind.

K: Well, good morning! OK, let's go!

R: Fear is fear. It all begins in the mind. Outward expressions of fear all begin in the mind. Just as all illness begins with emotions or thoughts before it manifests in the body. It begins the moment a soul enters the human body. That can be conception, it can be at the time of birth or anytime in between. The thoughts and emotions of the mother affect that soul. Then, the parents begin socializing, teaching, or programming (all the same) this young baby. Usually, this socializing is meant for the health and wellbeing of the child. Unfortunately, many times it is distorted. The distortion comes from the way the parents were socialized and it continues up and down the ancestral lineage. Before that child ever enters a school, its personality is formed. Then comes the programming from teachers, fellow students, siblings, friends until eventually bosses and spouses. To program a child to fit into a society that is completely dysfunctional is pure madness. Children are programmed to fit in. If they don't fit in, they are programmed with fear. Not fitting in or not belonging or just being different is akin to sin in your society. The thing is you all came to Earth to BE different! You came to be different but from day one you're told you're not good enough if you are different.

Even the best-meaning parents can't fight teachers, friends, co-workers, bosses, etc. Again, it is insidious. You came here to be different, yet when you express that individuality you are punished. It's no wonder people are filled with fear. They are constantly afraid to listen to their own souls. Their souls keep calling for them to learn the lessons, experience what they came here to experience and accomplish what they came to accomplish, but society fills them with fear if they listen to their soul's calling. They are filled with fear if they don't fit in, and the irony is that you were never supposed to fit in. Now do you see why Earth is considered one of the most difficult places to incarnate. Being on Earth is – well, to use your expression, like brushing your teeth while eating Oreos. That is a perfect analogy. You are trying to live your life brushing your teeth while society keeps feeding you Oreos. (Nothing against Oreos – this is just an easy and dramatic explanation) The trick of life is quit eating the cookie! No matter who is trying to force you to eat it. Listen to your soul fearlessly! It's why you're here. Think of an obstacle course. There will always be something in your way to slow you down, get in your way and try to stop you. If you see the prize at the end of the course, it is your inspiration to finish. The same is true of life. You came here for a specific reason, but you also set up the obstacles in your course called life. Those obstacles usually look like your parents, siblings, teachers, co-workers, or bosses. They are your obstacles to keep you from the finish line. Those same people can also be the ones on the sidelines cheering you on, giving you inspiration to reach your goal. It depends on what roles you choose those people to play in this life. Are they the obstacles or are they the cheerleaders? Sometimes they are both! You decided – they are merely doing what you asked of them this time around. Every time you reach an obstacle, it presents itself as fear. Your job is to figure out how to get over or work around the obstacle so you can reach your goal. The exact same thing is true in life. When fear-based thinking pops up in your life, ask yourself – is this merely another obstacle? If so, how do I get around it? Now fear-based thinking is very different from a warning. Let's talk about that another day.

K: Perfect. Thank you.

December 1, 2021

R: Let's continue today with warnings, shall we? Warnings are very different than fear, although people frequently confuse them. A true warning will elicit an almost automatic response in the mind and body. Fear based thinking happens after some thought comes into play with all the reasons why a certain thing shouldn't be done. Here are a few examples of warnings. Perhaps you are walking down the street and see that the pavement is uneven. The warning is immediate to pay attention, alter your walk or you could fall and hurt yourself. Fear-based thinking is that you won't go on a walk at all in case the pavement is uneven, and you might fall and hurt yourself. Another example is you're on vacation at the beach. There are signs posted that it is unsafe to swim that day, so you either go wading or sit on the sand and enjoy the view, the sun, and the fact you're on vacation. Fear-based thinking is that you either won't go to the beach at all because you're deathly afraid of sharks or you won't even go on vacation at all because you heard people have been eaten by sharks, drowned, or gotten so sunburned, they now have skin cancer.

Warnings are meant to give you a "heads up" indication. Warnings can and usually do trigger fear-based thinking. That's why warnings and fear are so frequently confused. Look at your life. Are you being smart about warnings? Warnings can come from other people or sources, or they can come from your own intuition. Start paying attention to where the warnings come from. Are they true or are they merely fear-based thoughts which have been triggered? I think you'll be amazed at how many so-called warnings are simply triggers for fear. Once you are aware of that you can also realize you have choices. Remain in fear or reprogram yourself to spot the difference and act accordingly. This may seem like a small step, but conscious thinking will change the world, not only your world.

December 4, 2021

R: Isn't it interesting that unconscious thought is what keeps us alive, yet we are discussing conscious thought. Unconscious thought is how we breathe and how the body heals itself. Conscious thought is freedom to choose.

K: So why don't people choose to thrive? Why don't people simply choose what is best for them; what is easiest for them, that they claim to want?

R: Because unconscious thought or previous programming is dominant. Past lives or better put other lives people have lived create fear which affects this life negatively. People get disappointed, they self-sabotage and give up on choosing what they want and how they live their lives because in their eyes and their experience it doesn't work out for them. It might work for others, but for some reason they deem themselves unworthy because their wants and needs are not being met. They have an entire history to prove it.

What people don't yet realize is that they need to go to the root of why they want what they want and why they're not getting it. It's rarely a straightforward answer. There are always three reasons why: 1 – false programming in this current life. 2 – a hangover of fear or failure from a past life or 3 – what they want doesn't serve their highest good and what they came here to accomplish in this lifetime. When people begin to investigate, by conscious thought, why they aren't getting what they want they can identify which of the three reasons is affecting them. It could be all three reasons! They can then make the conscious effort to clear past life energy and begin the process of reprogramming the false beliefs in their current life. One of the most important things is to realize what really does serve your healing and highest good this time around.

This sounds easy, and it actually is easy, but it can take a lifetime of conscious choices to get you to a place of emotional, physical, and spiritual thriving. That doesn't mean at the end of your life you've made it and its old garbage and programming up until then. Each and every day will get better and better once you decide consciously what it is that you really want and what you really need to make your life whole and balanced and abundant. It won't always feel like progress, but believe us, you are making progress. Think of how many decisions or choices you make in a day. Those are conscious choices. Now multiply that and you've got an idea of how many unconscious choices are really driving your behavior. Start there. Work with a qualified and skilled practitioner to help clear false programming from this life and fear-based thoughts and actions from past lives. Then you can begin making positive conscious choices in your current life for a thriving future for yourself.

December 6, 2021

K: Can we talk about UFOs and aliens today?

R: Are you calling me an alien? Ha! If the tin foil hat fits!

K: As you know I have had alien encounters most of my life.

R: True

K: Why me?

R: Why not you? And believe us, it's not just you. There are millions of living beings on your planet as well as on other planets who are being studied and used for the evolution of all. Please note, no one on your planet or elsewhere can be taken without a soul level agreement. That includes humans, animals, and plants. It also includes any being on any other planet.

K: Wow. I guess I never thought this would happen on other planets.

R: Humans have a hard time understanding anything that is not right in front of their faces. And sometimes not even then. That is the nature of humanity. It is also a reason for concern by those from other places in the galaxy for not every living being even lives on a planet! It's true. Some beings live on crafts. Some just exist. They don't need a – what you call – a brick and mortar place to go home to after a busy day at work. They just exist as energy.

K: Does energy have a home?

R: We know you listened to a video this morning about UFOs. One claim is that there are about 80 known "alien" species where reports have been done and sightings have been documented. There are actually many more. They are as yet unknown because they show up as pure energy. Humans do not have the technology or even capacity to capture images of that energy, but it does exist, nonetheless. What has been identified are several species who have contracts with planet Earth. There are countless other species who have contact with planets that are not Earth and are considered "alien" to the planet being visited. Earth, however, has the most attention right now because of the imbalance of energies. Your propensity for violence is concerning. Atomic and nuclear weaponry has the ability to not only destroy yourselves but the repercussions for any and every living thing is astronomical. Using atomic or nuclear bombs affects more than your so-called enemy. It will affect life on countless other planets. To use a human expression, it would be like shooting off your nose to spite your face.

K: So how do the peace lovers on Earth stop the madness?

R: Raise the vibration of the planet. That is why so many souls from many other planets are volunteering to come to Earth in human form. To assist in raising the vibration. Yes, we are deeply concerned. Many of these souls were finished with their lives on Earth and thought they'd never have to go back and yet they understand the urgency and have returned. Other souls are new to human life. They have the ability to have a profound impact on healing Earth as long as they don't get lost in the human experience.

K: What do you mean by that?

R: Think of it this way. Many humans agree to being a police officer as their way to earn a living and help keep the peace in their community. Most do exactly that. But there are a few who succumb to the pressures of corrupt organizations and take bribes, turn a blind eye, or simply can't take the pressure of the job and are emotionally unbalanced. Those are what you call the bad apples - they spoil it for all those around them. That's what it is like for some souls from elsewhere. They come to Earth to help keep the peace but for various reasons and pressures become the human energy they swore to protect and serve. Only now have they become the reason help is needed, rather than the actual help. That is how difficult Earth can be for any soul entering the denseness of the planet.

K: I know that's the reason I am here – to protect and serve. I feel like I almost failed on a galactic scale but found my balance relatively late in life.

R: You are a hybrid. Half human DNA and half a mixture of alien DNA. You are what we laughingly call a multi-tasker. You are on Earth to help raise the vibration by helping other humans find themselves. You are also in human form to help your own soul evolve. You came onto the planet with pure intent and a job to do. From the minute were born "life" got in the way. You began to act out in anger in an effort to fit in with other humans. It took years for you to regain the knowledge of why you came to Earth. Can you now understand how hard it is for those souls who are not hybrids to acclimate?

K: OK. Help me understand. If all human souls are seeded from other planets, how can they not be hybrids too? Aren't we all hybrids?

R: While that is true to a degree, it's a bit more complicated than that.

K: Can we discuss that later?

R: Absolutely.

December 8, 2021

K: Thank you for picking up where we left off on Monday.

R: It is our pleasure. Did you get the clarification during your massage on Monday?

K: I certainly did – thank you! Here's what I remember. Correct me if I'm wrong. It's true all humans are seeded from other planets, hybrids are simply humans that have been bred, if you will, from two or more planets. They have been bred or combined in what you would call an artificial way to create a new kind of human.

R: You currently are doing the same with your pets, your plants, etc. Labradoodle? Genes from a Labrador and Poodle. One isn't better than another - just different. The same is true of humans, so please keep your egos in check. Hybrid humans are bred to have traits to raise the vibration of the planet more quickly, but to do it in different ways.

K: Such as?

R: To put it in a rudimentary way so you can understand, one hybrid group is sent to Earth to discover ways to eliminate your trash, garbage, waste, etc. Another group is sent to work out different ways of healing. Another is to create alternate ways to use or create power. By power we mean the power you use to run your car, your electrical gadgets, your furnaces, etc. Another group is sent to work with water – how to convert sea water into drinking water.

K: Ok, I get it. What about in my case? I know I'm a hybrid, but I also know I have a hybrid daughter who is not on planet Earth. I talk about this in my book *We Are Not Alone: My Extraterrestrial Contact.*

R: You are another level of hybridization, but not all that unusual. You are a hybrid of two different planetary genomes. You are most definitely on Earth to raise the vibration. We were getting concerned about your ability to activate, so we gave you a little push. Do you remember?

K: How could I forget?! You pushed me into a brick wall! 37 stiches later and I looked like a mummy.

R: Well, yes. Sorry about that but it seemed to be the only way to get your attention.

K: Yes, well it worked.

R: Indeed

K: How about my daughter?

R: She was bred to work on other planets. She is a high-ranking officer in her fleet. We are very excited about her success. As you know, she does have much human in her, but enough other DNA to be able to not only survive other atmospheres but to be able to thrive. You don't remember, but you have met her on several occasions. You only remember meeting her once when she was a young child, but the two of you have met briefly on several other occasions. You are as proud as any other human parent.

K: What planet do I originate from and what planet does she originate from?

R: They are not exactly planets but are star systems which have yet to be identified by your astronomers and scientists.

K: So why do I have a memory of living on a pink planet?

R: Because that was your first home. It is not where you were born or how you were created. It is impossible to explain something to you when you have no concept. We are trying to communicate these things to you in a way and with words you do understand. The English language, as with any language, is very limited. Because you are a hybrid it is easier for you to communicate with us. Most humans aren't wired that way. You are. That's why you are part of this program – to listen, write it down, ask questions, put it into a readable format so others can get the same messages you're getting but through human communication rather than "alien" communication which most humans are highly resistant to.

K: Sorry it took me so long to catch on.

R: No worries. You're doing it now. The timing is perfect.

December 11, 2021

K: I don't have a topic in mind today, so the floor is yours.

R: Let's talk about animals.

K: Wow, ok.

R: Particularly let's talk about your domesticated animals, such as dogs, cats, birds, etc.

K: I've often wondered if our animals are really aliens.

R: We find that humorous because it is true. They are indeed aliens, as are you. Animals were also seeded from other planets. There were so many species sent here. Some survived and some didn't. What you see today are the survivors. Some of your so-called pets were made to and agreed to be domesticated. Others preferred to be feral. Just like humans, some of you prefer to be inside and pampered others outside but still cared for, and others prefer living in the wild, outside of human contact. Here's what we are noticing; people are so lonely for love, acceptance, and peace that they think they get it from their pets since they can't seem to find it in other humans. Don't misunderstand. Love is love. If people want to give and get love from pets, we applaud that. But if they are substituting human love for pet love, that is concerning. Humans can have and need love from each other. It's when they avoid human contact because of pets that needs to be addressed.

K: I have to say I'm feeling weird about this subject. People seem to be more protective and defensive about their pets than they are about their children. I feel like talking about this is treading on rocky ground.

R: And talking about the destruction of your planet isn't? Do we detect some avoidance here?

K: Yes, People are so sensitive and defensive about themselves, their families, and their pets. I don't want anyone to miss the other really important messages in this book.

R: Hmm, is someone living in fear?

K: Ha, yeah, I guess so.

R: We applaud love in any form. Love between any living thing is wonderful. Please don't misunderstand. We are not asking anyone to give up their family pets. What we are trying to point out is many people use their pets as a deterrent to face the issues of why they came to the planet. Who wouldn't want a playful puppy around the house? Who wouldn't want a darling kitten curled up in your lap? That is not the point. The point is people came to this planet to evolve. They do this by learning lessons. When people use pets as a way to avoid learning those lessons, they need to realize that they will keep coming back to Earth until they embrace the lessons they came here to learn.

People can and do learn from pets, too. Pets can be the best teachers of what love looks like and help us learn the lessons we came here to learn. Pets are wonderful! Don't misread or misunderstand.

All life forms are sacred. We love it when certain souls create pet rescues. Even zoos, when properly designed, are good. They become another tool for learning. Perhaps we should be more specific; anything people use to avoid learning the lessons they came here to learn needs to be addressed. Today we are specifically talking about other living creatures labeled pets.

K: So really avoidance is today's topic – not just pets.

R: Correct. Pets are just one-way humans use to avoid. We love and respect all life forms. So don't get your feathers ruffled by this topic. Connection to any living soul is beautiful. We're just asking you to be aware that your pets are there to help you evolve, not keep you from evolving. Just like any other thing in life. Use your connections and experiences to learn and evolve, not to avoid. Avoidance is fear really.

December 12, 2021

K: I still feel uncomfortable about our last discussion.

R: Why?

K: Because people are so sensitive about their pets.

R: People are so sensitive about anything and everything. Why should discussion about pets be any different?

K: It just feels like we may have crossed a line.

R: What if we did? Did we cross a line with them, or did we cross a line with you?

K: I don't know. Perhaps the line was crossed with me since I'm the one bristling when this information hasn't even been presented publicly, yet.

R: There you go! Give others the opportunity to embrace, ignore, or reject any of the material we are presenting. We ask that you present the material as it was given to you. Please do not alter the material to fit your personal beliefs or limitations. Please leave that up to the reader. We love that you are asking questions. In fact, we can't wait for more of your inquiries. Ask away! But please do not alter the messages we are delivering to you.

K: OK, thank you for the clarification. I will not add my personal opinions and will promise to deliver the messages exactly as you are giving them to me.

R: We thank you. Also, why do you think we picked you for this project? We trust that you will do as we ask. You always claim that you want things for the greater good. Here is your opportunity. The messages we are bringing through you to those on your planet are indeed for the greater good. It is up to you to let it flow.

K: Thank you. That takes some pressure off.

R: You will also find that when you enter this information digitally into your computer additional downloads will be given to clarify the subject a bit more.

K: Thank you. I appreciate that.

R: And we appreciate you.

K: I just got a flash of something I'd like your input on.

R: Please, ask.

K: Several years ago, I had an experience of being on a craft working with my teacher. I was being shown horrible images but also the group of people I was to help – "save," if you will. I was also told that I would know what to do when the time was right. My question is this – are you that teacher?

R: Very astute of you! Yes, I am that teacher.

K: Is the time now? Is this book what is going to help "save" people?

R: Yes! The time is now. As we discussed earlier, your planet is in crisis mode. People need to be rescued. But your job is to rescue them emotionally and spiritually. Others are there to rescue physically.

I use the word rescue deliberately after our pet conversation. People are claiming to "rescue" their pets just because they came from a shelter. Did they ever stop to think that their pet rescued them? The pet has now learned a different way to be treated and a different way to act. The rescuers have also adapted the way they act as well as altering their own belief system. This happens mostly for the good but there are and always will be those who warp or distort the real reason for animal adoption. The pet picks the person, and the person picks the pet. After that, it is up to both to figure out how it plays out.

The same is true with this book. You are the person presenting the material and it is up to the general population or who picks up the information, who reads it, and who acts on the messages offered. It is more dramatic to say you are rescuing and saving people when we all know people save and rescue themselves. But it takes people like you to give them that opportunity. Think back to when Neale Donald Walsch's book *Conversations with God* came into public consciousness. It saved you, didn't it?

K: Yes, in a way. Saved is kind of a strong word, however. It helped clarify what I believed but couldn't articulate. It was a huge step in my own soul's evolution. Most of his books had that effect on me.

R: So, he presented information and whomever was to find it – did. The same is true of an artist, a musician, and inventor. They all receive information from spirit whether they realize it or not. They present it to the world. The souls meant to find it – will. It's as simple as that. It is true for anyone tapped into spirit. They listen and then using their human gifts present it to the world. You are doing exactly the same thing. You have tapped into us, the collective. You are listening, downloading the information, and using your gift of writing and discipline and are presenting it to the world. Whomever buys it, reads it, and learns from it is supposed to – is ready to make changes in their belief system and perhaps even act on it using their gifts and talents to help the greater good. Isn't it a marvelous chain of events?

Initially we got your attention by saying you would be saving people. While that is still true, we want you to think of it now a bit differently. You are presenting powerful information so people who are ready can and will save themselves and others and eventually your planet. A cosmic ripple effect.

K: Let me ask you this; am I teaching people correctly when I talk about the difference between being a victim, being a survivor, and thriving?

R: Yes, you are to a large extent. In your society people do have choices also known as free will so we always wonder why they would choose anything other than thriving. We do want to be clear that in some societies everybody thrives. In other societies, that choice is taken away, but in the society in which you live almost everybody has a choice. So, why do they pick victimhood or merely surviving?

K: That's my question to you!

R: Much depends on the lessons they came here to learn in this lifetime. Did they perhaps choose to be a victim? Did they choose to just get by or survive? Those are usually the two places of being where the hardest lessons are learned. If everybody thrived where would be those difficult lessons? People choose families, friends, and situations which set them up perfectly to learn those lessons. It's how people react to those situations when they get here. Perhaps going from victim to survivor is the biggest lesson they'll learn in any lifetime. In many cases, thriving without first surviving not only doesn't teach lessons but can create a person without compassion or empathy. They must first come from a place of being a victim or barely surviving to eventually thriving. This can happen in one lifetime, or it might take many, many lifetimes.

Can you see how you are still judging people?

K: Gulp. Yes. I can see that now.

R: Your heart is in the right place wanting to give tools to people so they can all thrive, but you can also be quick to judge when they don't listen, stay stuck, or choose another way. After all, how long did it take you to begin to thrive?

K: Ok, you got me there.

R: You've spent most of your life as a victim or just surviving. It was only when those lessons were learned that you chose to thrive. We love the work you're doing – don't get us wrong – this is just another piece of clarity for your own growth as well as in the way you approach others. Don't automatically assume people are ready to thrive. Even if they are, it can take years, even decades for that change to happen. It can also happen overnight when that shift in thinking happens suddenly. People will change if and when they are ready. You cannot or should not judge when that is. People come to you for a reason. You give them some tools to help them attain the changes they say they want to make. Here's the kicker what they say they want and what they truly want can be diametrically opposed. Your job is to work with compassion, patience, and empathy. It is then up to your client how they want to or don't want to use the tools you give them. You are not the judge. You are the guide, teacher, and emotional caretaker. This is just a gentle reminder that when you teach people not to judge, you need to occasionally look in the mirror. If you do this your job will become even more fun than it already is. You come from a place of love. Deliver information you believe to be true and then you leave it to the recipient to do what they will with it. You always say that when you give someone a gift, there are no strings attached. Your work is a gift. Give it with the same energy. No expectations in return. No strings attached. We love the work you're doing.

December 16, 2021

K: Can we talk about jealousy today?

R: Sure. Why do you ask?

K: I think I'd like to talk about all the Earthly emotions. We've talked about love so now I'd like to address some of the others, starting with jealousy. I remember experiencing jealousy as a youth but now I no longer do and am pretty excited about that!

R: You should be! Congratulations! Jealousy can be interpreted as if they have something I don't. Why do they have the thing? Usually, it is an external item of some kind – and I don't. They then get jealous because they believe there isn't enough of the "thing" to go around. They immediately go into a place of lack or what is actually fear. They have "it" so now I can't have "it." I was robbed! I'm fearful that now my needs won't be met because they were delivered to someone else. And how dare that other person be happy when they know I wanted "it" and they stole it from me. They must be a greedy and awful person.

A better way to look at this situation is if someone else gets what you want. Look at it with gratitude. Obviously "it" exists which means it can exist for you too! Instead of jealousy be grateful. That person showed you that whatever "it" was that you were wishing for and wanting does actually exist. They are the proof. Thank them instead of being jealous. They just gave you permission to manifest the same thing for yourself. Now it's up to you to allow it into your life too. Can you feel the difference in the vibration? Jealousy/fear is a very low vibrating energy which slows down everything. Love, appreciation, and gratitude are high vibrations which speed things up bringing to you what you want. This is true of all the other emotions you want to discuss. There is only love and fear. If it's not love it is fear just disguised as jealousy, hate, greed, apathy, and anger. All the fear emotions tell us that the person has chosen to be a victim in that situation or in their life as a whole. Choosing to be a victim is telling the world you are afraid. Again, your society applauds that. They want victims – people living in fear. Remember people living in fear are much easier to control. And that's what the game is all about. Control. Once individuals take control of their own lives, their own happiness, it is much harder to control them. People are constantly threatened with shame, fear, even death if they don't buy the next product, live the way they are expected to live. Those who are awakened know the difference. That's what being awakened means. You are aware of all the madness around you, and it has little to no effect on you or your behavior or the choices you make. Even with the threat of a fate worse than death? (We love that one by the way)

Death is beautiful. Death is waking up from the dream of life on Earth. Awakened people know that the threat of death means nothing. It doesn't change who they are one iota. They are energy. They are love; that energy is housed in a human body, that's all. Awakened people understand they are on planet Earth to learn, experience, and accomplish. Even the really hard lessons are understood. They are still painful, but awakened people understand that beneath the pain lies love, growth, and understanding. They know that everything on Earth is temporary, and no one can put the fear in them of not being enough or even dying. They can't die. It is impossible. The body can stop functioning, but the soul is eternal, strong and without fear. It simply is.

The soul is ever evolving. Knowing that and embracing that is being awakened. Those souls understand that we are all one. We ARE created equal. We've just chosen different experiences from each other. No soul is better than or less than any other soul. We are the same. We are one. When they win – you win. When they hurt – you hurt. It's whether you choose to acknowledge it or not. Just because you choose not to acknowledge that fact doesn't make it not exist. Embrace every emotion on Earth. That is why you came. Once you experience them awaken to the thought that love is really the only emotion which serves you. Then you can help others stuck in the other emotions to awaken too. It is up to them whether to hear the messages or not. We cannot judge them for their choices for we know not why they are here or what they chose to learn in their Earth experience. Yes, go out and teach but do not judge those who do not listen or learn. Perhaps that is why they are here. That is why they are here – to NOT listen. To NOT learn from you. Teach – do not judge. Those that came here to learn from you will find you. When we use the word you, we do mean you, but we also mean every other soul on your planet. Every soul is a teacher with a message. Are you choosing to listen to them?

December 17, 2021

K: We are nearing the holidays. Yesterday I noticed all the people out and about getting ready to celebrate. What I didn't notice was a change in people's energy. Many didn't get to spend time with friends and family last year because of Covid. This year Covid is still here and supposedly as strong or stronger than ever. People are still acting frenetic like last year didn't happen at all. Why?

R: Good question – why? Why indeed? A pandemic where people are forced to sequester was/is the perfect opportunity to reevaluate their lives. To closely look at what's working for them and what isn't and then plan for changes. That is happening for many by mostly letting go of what they don't want but not figuring out what they do want. So many lives have been lost during this time – the pandemic and myriad other reasons. This year during the holidays those gathered together will miss and acknowledge their loved one's absence but will not have made any significant changes in their own behavior or their own lives. That is why you don't sense a shift in energy as you are out and about. There hasn't been a change. Not a significant one anyway. People have basically or are in the process of picking up where they left off. They complain about what is going on. Yes, they are grateful to be able to gather again. They will celebrate being with friends and family, but again no significant change in thoughts or behavior.

K: That makes me sad.

R: It should. Every day is a new day to make the change people insist they want to make yet never do. Even when a pandemic appears forcing change in thoughts and behavior people can't wait to get back to life as normal again so they can go back to complaining about the madness. They are right about one thing – it certainly is madness. But again, yours is a free will planet, you make choices every minute of every day. Each moment is an opportunity for significant change – to exercise free will, to create the change people say they want. Here's the kicker – most people don't know what they want. They want others to make the changes for them which will make their lives easier. When those changes happen people still complain that it isn't enough, or it isn't what they really wanted. Only when people take control of their own lives will there be significant change that matters. Quit looking to others to make those changes for you. Only YOU can make the changes which will have a significant impact on the way you live your life. But if you are the one in charge of your life, there is no one to blame right? If you let someone else make the changes you can blame and point fingers all day long. People are afraid to take control of their own lives. What if "it" doesn't turn out right? Who can they blame? What if "it" does turn out right? Who will judge them? It's a vicious circle based on fear. This is just another way fear rules people.

If a pandemic isn't enough to get people to look inside themselves, what is? When is enough enough? Enough is a place different for each person. Only they know if and when enough fear is enough. That's what makes your planet so wonderful and so special and so difficult. It is up to each individual soul to make decisions affecting their experience on this planet. See? They are making choices! Sometimes the choice is to do nothing. That is still a choice. People don't realize it, but they ARE making choices in their lives every minute of every day even if that choice is to do nothing or that choice is to "go with the flow" or that choice is to complain about how messed up their lives are. It's still free will. It's still people making decisions and choices. What would be lovely is if they made those choices from a place of consciousness and power. Choice is choice. It is up to you. Do you choose to blame others for your lot in life or do you choose to recognize where that choice really originated? It originated within you! When you recognize that, it is the key to change yourself, your life, your planet. It all starts with you! Take the time to look around you. There are teachers everywhere. It is your opportunity to open your eyes, make the decision to change and then decide what those changes are. There are teachers who will help and guide you. Sometimes those teachers help clarify what you don't want. Some teachers are there to show you what you do want. Still and always, the choice is yours.

December 20, 2021

K: I just finished an online course where the last lesson was that anything is possible. We were to write what we wanted and to know if it's possible. I want a healthy planet where there is no violence. A planet where human love and respect exist for all living things. Is that possible?

R: Not only is it possible it already exists! It just isn't Earth.

K: I know that! I want all those things for planet Earth and for me to experience all those things while I'm on planet Earth. Is that possible?

R: Yes, it is possible but unlikely.

K: Why?

R: How could you learn the lessons you came here to learn if everything was as you say? That's why souls come to Earth in the first place – because of violence, lust, hate, greed, jealousy. That's what makes the Earth so difficult. That's why it is "the" place to go when souls want to evolve in a particular manner. If the Earth was peaceful, respectful, clean, etc. The soul wouldn't be able to learn in a particular way, live in a particular way, and experience in a particular way.

K: So when I hear anything is possible, that isn't really true, is it?

R: It is true – just not for planet Earth at this time. What is true is that you can live that way in your own life. Live without violence. Live with respect for all other living things. Live with peace in your mind, body, heart, and soul. If that is what you truly want, start with you. Make it possible for you. Lead by example. Also, remember, not everyone comes to Earth with the same reasoning that you did. Some come wanting to experience violence, hate, fear, lack of respect for themselves or anyone else. That is a lesson, too. It is just as important for soul evolution as the peaceful lessons you came here to learn. You are judging others again when you state violence is wrong. It is merely another lesson in the human experience.

It's the same as judging someone who prefers the nighttime to the daytime. Both serve a purpose. Both provide lessons. Isn't non-judgment one of the lessons you came here to learn? Here is another reminder of how judging manifests.

K: Ouch. Looks like I've been schooled.

R: Isn't that why you're here? To be schooled?

December 22, 2021

R: Let's talk about the weather today.

K: Ok. That seems to be a topic of conversation whenever and wherever.

R: Have you noticed some rather interesting weather patterns lately?

K: Yes, actually a lack of patterns. It's the end of December and we've really had no snow to speak of other than less than an inch a few weeks ago and that was mostly gone in a day. *(This is in the Midwest of the United States)*

R: The hot topic is climate change. Most people agree that it is destroying your planet. They are wrong, as your friend who has studied climate change for many years claims. The weather patterns are cyclical. Patterns just go back before records were kept so there is no way to prove what's happening now is cyclical. Man is destroying your planet. That much is true, but it can't always be blamed on climate change. As the climate does change, as it always has on your planet. From its birth, continents will appear and disappear as the Earth shifts to adapt. This is natural and as it should be. What isn't natural is the way humans react to this change and the way they are destroying their own home in a way that has nothing to do with climate change. But they blame so much of what is going on on climate change. Another level of insanity. You are shooting yourselves in the foot and then blaming your neighbor. Any logical person can see this, but with your government, politicians, and media, they try to make you believe otherwise. If they say it loud enough and often enough people believe. That's exactly what is happening now. It's not the climate. Well, part of it is the climate but it is behaving as it should and as it always has. If you are looking to blame someone, blame yourselves for believing what is fed to you. You are poisoning your mind and your bodies. Your souls know the truth. You're being fed propaganda to not trust your souls. Your souls know the truth. It's time to trust again. Trust your souls. Trust your light. Trust that inner voice. There is conflict between what you hear on the outside and what you hear from the inside – from your soul. Listen to your soul! It will never fail you. Let the weather do what it will. Your Earth is shifting as it should. To clarify, climate change is cyclical – global warming is not. Climate change is a natural part of Earth's evolution. Global warming is completely caused by man. Your human behaviors are speeding things up. That you do have control over. That is where the focus should be. Human behavior. As in all things it always comes down to you. Who are you? What do you want?

December 24, 2021

K: Merry Christmas Eve! Why do we celebrate Christmas? I mean it's supposed to be the birth of Christ, but many people know that isn't the actual anniversary of that day.

R: Let's go to Shakespeare. A rose by any other name would smell as sweet. In this case the day isn't important – just celebrate. You don't necessarily even have to celebrate the birth of Jesus. Jesus is appreciative but doesn't demand or wish it. This is another human thing – just like Santa. Who says Santa isn't real? If he is alive in people's imaginations, hearts, and souls then he is alive and does exist. The same with anything. If it exists within you then it exists. Go ahead and celebrate however you choose and whenever you choose. The key here is celebration! Many families celebrate on days other than Christmas. Does that make it wrong? Absolutely not. They are making the effort to be together and enjoy each other by celebrating. We really should celebrate every day. On your Thanksgiving and Christmas holidays you express gratitude for friends and family, the food you eat, etc. Why don't you do that every day? Why wait until a so-called holiday?

With your friends or without them be grateful. Gratitude is everything. Jesus loves you celebrating his birthday because he loves to see the joy, togetherness, and the gratitude, but mostly the celebration. He also wants you to know that you can do this any day – every day – whenever you choose. Whatever works for you. If you want to use his birthday as the excuse to do this – he celebrates your decision and wishes his birthday was every day, not for himself but for you to live in gratitude – every day not just Christmas.

December 26, 2021

R: Take a day of rest today. You have a lot on your mind.
We'll continue tomorrow.

K: I'd like to ask you a couple of questions today.

R: We already know what they are but go ahead and ask anyway. Ha!

K: I know you are the voice of the collective, but will I ever get to know the other members of the collective?

R: There are many of us so, no, you will not get to know all of us as individual souls. You will, however, get to know several of us representing individual souls or better still representing areas of expertise. They will come forward as appropriate.

K: Will they come forward through our writings or through my voice?

R: Both.

K: Yikes, when will that happen?

R: Again, it will happen as appropriate.

K: And you are the one to determine that?

R: We, including you, will determine that.

K: Ok. My second question has to do with what happened during a reading last week. As I was doing energy work with a client, I started speaking in the third person. That has never happened before. It felt normal-not scary at all but still a bit surprising. Was that you or was it someone else from the collective?

R: Your client was open to it and would not be frightened, so we chose her and we chose that particular time when you would be off guard, wouldn't be scared, and we could experience what it would feel like to channel. It was three of us.

K: Your timing was good!

R: We know.

K: I'd really like to give permission before you just take over my body.

R: We didn't just take over your body. We had your permission. You just don't remember. Again, to keep you from being anxious or scared.

K: Ok. As long as I give permission in some way.

R: Always

K: When we first connected a year ago. You said this would happen - that I would begin to verbally channel you.

R: Correct, except we didn't actually mention it to you until October of this year.

K: True. I forgot. So, will this now happen more frequently?

R: If you choose.

K: Will the channeling be for individual clients or for groups of people?

R: It will be for both. However, we want you to get used to us integrating with you so it will be with individual clients for now – and randomly at that. When you are ready, we will begin to gather small groups where you can speak on a more global level rather than on an individual level.

K: I'm ok with that. I would like to know who else, other than you, will be coming through. I'd like to learn their names. or what they prefer to be called.

R: Yes, that will happen.

K: Thank you. That's all I have for now. Goodbye.

January 4, 2022

K: Why do so many people make New Year's resolutions and then break them in three months or less?

R: Because people fight change, especially within themselves. They don't like who they are, but they don't like the unknown even more. The devil you know cliché is perfect for your question.

People must change their habits. Those habits they really don't like, or they wouldn't want to change them in the first place. There are usually so many things they don't like that they attempt to change them all at once. They only make it harder on themselves when they do it that way. They set themselves up for failure and don't even realize that's what they're doing. They think it's for success but it's really a failure in their eyes.

They think the new year is the only time to commit to change instead of thinking each day-each minute is an opportunity for change. So, let's say when someone has a weight loss goal. First, what is their motive? Is it to "look good" by society's standards? Is it to "get healthy" when they really don't know what that means?

Motive is the number one reason people don't achieve what they want. They are doing it for someone or something outside themselves. The number two reason is they set goals too high. I'm going to lose 50 pounds! Instead, don't think of 50 pounds this year. Perhaps 1 pound this month. Instead of going to the gym every day, perhaps begin with 1-2 days per week. Want to eat healthier? Add 1 fruit or 1 Vegetable per day. Don't throw out all of the junk food. You'll just end up buying it all over again and then feel like a failure.

Is your goal to "get organized"? Don't look at the entire home or office. You'll get overwhelmed. Pick one room. In that room, pick one drawer, one cupboard, or one closet. Begin with one. First, ask yourself the question, "why do I want to get organized?" Is it because you want to change the way you live? Is it so you don't feel embarrassed if guests come over? Look first at the why of your goal. It must come from inside yourself not outside yourself.

People begin with the attitude that change is temporary. Once I clean the closet, I'll go back to my old way of throwing things in the closet and slamming the door shut. It's more of a "let's get this over with" kind of resolution, so I can go back to my old, comfortable way of living.

In your society people are programmed to look outside themselves. That should be the goal for every human being on Earth; to look inside.

R: They need to teach that in your schools. To look inside yourself! It's not just meditation. It's not just quieting the mind although those are all essential. It is critical thinking. What is good for the individual, the tribe, the country, and the planet? Once that is realized then the individual can decide how they want to show up or express themselves within that critical thinking.

Your society is losing the art of critical thinking. Instead, they are being told what is right and what is wrong. They are being led to act in a certain way to make them easier to control. It always begins with questioning your motive. Is what you want to do because it is for your healing and best and highest good or is it because of what you think others expect of you or even what you think you should expect of yourself? Because usually your healing and highest good is also the country's, and the planet's healing and highest good. Remember we are all one.

January 21,2022

K: I haven't written for a few days because I haven't felt the push from you. Are you giving me a break, giving yourself a break, or are we done?

R: We are far from done, my friend. It's been the holidays for you, so we wanted you to take some time and enjoy them as well as rest and rejuvenate.

K: Thank you. I was a bit worn out. It's been a busy year.

R: Yes, and get ready for more activity. 2022 will be a year of extremes. Extreme for you and many people.

K: I must ask you – I had a dream a few nights ago which really disturbed me. A tornado came and lifted my house off its foundation. The house remained intact but was balancing on a fence. Just when I realized that both I and the house were ok, a Tsunami came rushing through the windows. I heard flooding and it looked like pictures of any Tsunami I've ever seen. My question is this: Was this just a dream? Was this precognitive? Was it foretelling of disasters for Earth? Was it a warning for my personal life?

R: That is certainly more than one question! But we do understand. The answer is yes to all of your questions. Yes, it was a dream. Yes, it was precognitive. The way you usually receive dreams is the truth but presented in a unique way, Correct?

K: True.

R: It is a warning of what's ahead for Earth. Continued natural disasters. This is part of the natural cycle of things. The last time the Earth shifted like this however, it was not as populated. Therefore, not as many lives and homes were lost. There was also no record keeping so this all seems new to the human race. It is new to the human race. It's just not new to Earth. Now, the rate the natural disasters are happening is accelerated by human behavior, this is new to the equation. As for your life personally? Yes, it will be extreme for you. You may even be knocked off your foundation, but as you recall, you were fine in your dream. Water from floods or a tsunami represents emotions for you. It will be a flood of emotion for you personally. Extremely happy and extremely sad. You are preparing for another shift, just as the Earth is.

K: Those shifts always knock us off our foundation, don't they?

R: Typically, yes. Water also represents emotions for the Earth. The Earth cries tears for its change and shifting, too. Change can be difficult for individuals, as well as the Earth itself. It happens. Surround change with love rather than fear and see and feel the difference. Embrace the changes the Earth makes.

K: How do we do that?

R: Like any change. What is the gift in this? What am I to learn from this? How can I pass this onto others for their awakening? How do I learn from this? Begin by treating your Earth - your home - with more respect. Love it, be grateful for it and treat it the way you wish to be treated, for the Earth is a living breathing thing just as you are.

January 25, 2022

K: I am back, but as you know I've got a lot going on right now.

R: Who do you think is sending these opportunities to you? We are! You're ready to begin speaking and the messages we're giving you will be an important part of your talks.

K: Yes, boss.

R: Ha. Very funny. The collective is here rolling their eyes at you.

K: I think it's timely to discuss conspiracy theories, don't you?

R: That is correct. Conspiracy theories always begin with a thread of truth which is why so many people believe them. They are, however, started by highly creative, intelligent but angry people. They love the "us against them" way of life and conspiracy theories are a perfect way to ignite the flames of anger and victimhood. There is enough truth with proof to get others to believe, follow, and continue to spread the diatribe. The initiators of these theories are creative and intelligent, which is also why people believe them. They position the truth in such a way that it inflames hurt, anger, and victim mentality in their followers. Once the initial "truth" is out, is when the trouble begins. That's when the truth becomes a yarn. It becomes bigger, longer, louder with no one now questioning anything because they have proof of the initial theory so everything else must be correct, too. As you already know, there is light and dark in everything and every person. Anybody can take the dark and exaggerate it and twist it in a way to serve their own needs. The initial dark statement might have been true, but it was only true from the perspective of the person initiating the story. The reverse is also true. You can take the light in anybody and exaggerate that, too. It is called the halo effect and is usually used only on those who are no longer with us. Again, the halo effect is only from the perspective of the person who initiates that thought.

Either way, when you demonize someone or something, it creates an "us against them" energy. One side is the hero, and the other side is the victim. Who wins? Nobody. With conspiracy theories, nobody is right 100% of the time. Conspiracy theories are always based on fear, not love. We don't care what side of the theory you're on, it is fear-based. Is it your goal to live from fear or live from love? It is again, your choice – just like everything else in your life. If you choose fear, you are not wrong.

Perhaps fear is one of the lessons you came to Earth to experience. If you choose love, you are not wrong, either. Is that what you came to Earth to experience? We will say that your soul came to Earth to evolve and eventually attain enlightenment. We hope in the end, you will all choose love, but we do understand that choosing fear is part of the journey too. So, you see, you choose – always. But, if your choice is layered with judgement of any kind towards another, then you really are still choosing to fear, no matter which side of theory you stand.

You see even if you are on the non-believing side of any theory and still judge the believing side, you are choosing to fear just as strongly. When you choose love, there are no sides. Hero/victim, "us against them" no longer exists. If we are all one, it would be like you saying your left foot is wrong and your right foot is indeed right. You need both. Both are part of the whole. Both, working together, make the whole-body function more smoothly. If one foot is working against the other foot, the whole body suffers. It's that simple.

January 29, 2022

K: Yes, I have been avoiding you, sorry. The world is in such a weird place right now that I'm finding it difficult to pick up my pen and get more news from you about the state of the world.

R: We understand. The problems of the world are overwhelming. It will take generations to fix what is wrong. After all, it took generations to get you where you are today. When we discuss problems on Earth, we don't expect you to fix what's wrong. We expect you to take care of you and help us get the word out. If everybody took care of themselves, as well as the children they bring into the world, that would be enough. But people aren't always willing to do that. Some are not able to do that. That's where others step up as part of their journey on Earth – to help others, in addition to themselves.

It really is simple. Take care of yourself and take care of those who are unable to take care of themselves. The problem lies with those who expect to be taken care of, when they really can function and take care of themselves. It also begins with those who feel like they never have enough. More, more, more, and still they want more. When is enough enough? In their effort to have more they'll exploit others. In an effort to have enough, the others will have to obey. They do this for a few reasons – to survive, out of ignorance, or because they don't care. People have been conditioned or raised by others with the same belief system. That's why it's taken generations to get to where you are today.

It takes people who are happy and thriving to shift the survival mentality that exists today. Please note that when we use the word thrive, we don't necessarily mean rich. We mean happy. To thrive is to be happy with who you are, the people you surround yourselves with, and the work that you do. Sounds simple, doesn't it? It is simple until the balance is so off kilter that you have most people in survival mode. Even if the wealthy gave away their money, you would be in a similar situation. You see those who are merely surviving need to be taught what it looks like and feels like to thrive. Right now, they see rich and poor.

They don't know the difference between survive and thrive. Even many of your wealthy people are still in a survival mindset. They feel like they never have enough. Isn't that the exact same thing as the belief system of the poor? There is never enough. That's what needs to change for people to thrive. To be happy. When people are happy, they know they have enough, and the universe will always provide enough. That's how it's meant to be. That's the way it's set up to be. When people are happy, they share wealth- food, clothing, shelter, because they understand that the universe will always provide those things for them so they can freely give, share, and create for others. Simple?

February 9, 2022

K: I had a thought while on my walk the other day. In the divisive world we live in, no matter what your opinion is, there is evidence to back you up. Where does this "evidence" come from? What sources can we actually believe?

R: Ah HA! Critical thinking! You are correct in noticing that people can "prove" their theories with so-called evidence. This evidence usually comes from the internet, news on the television, newspapers, friends, and books. What is the source of any or all these sources? Human beings. A human is stating an opinion. That's really all any of it is. The level of opinion varies depending on the level of experience of the person reporting the so-called facts.

Even if facts are reported accurately, people hear and process through their own level of experience. In other words, they hear what they want to hear. Is your real question, is this wrong?

K: I guess so.

R: What is wrong with hearing what you want to hear? People do it in everything. You've noticed that in your own work, haven't you?

K: Oh yes, for sure!

R: What people choose to hear and how they choose to process that information will almost always support the rest of their decisions which is to be a victim, a survivor, or a thriver.

K: That seems to be true. But is that what I'm choosing to hear?

R: Why, yes, it is.

K: When I work with clients and am attempting to get them to understand their own lives – their own choices, I do get varied responses. Some people respond as the victim and start beating themselves up for the choices they've made. They also start pointing fingers at those people who they feel wronged them.

Other people freeze. The task of reprogramming themselves seems daunting. They don't know where to start even though I've just given them the tools to do so, yet they do nothing.

The third group is usually so ready for change, and they want control over their lives, they just don't know how to begin. They are the thrivers. I give them the tools. The light bulb goes off in their heads and they are off to the races.

R: All are not ready. Think back to 45 years ago. Were you ready for what you know today?

K: Oh, heavens no. Not even a little.

R: Well then. Why do you expect it of others? That's what is hurting your energy. Not your clients, but your own expectations. Remember, it always circles back to you. Always in all ways.

K: You are right, of course. Thank you for that reminder.

B: Blessings to you, dear one.

February 26,2022

K: I heard something remarkably interesting yesterday. I was with a client, and I saw what appeared to be a member of clergy standing by her. This gentleman was dressed in a similar way to the pope but without the miter. I asked my client if she was Catholic or had a strong connection to any member of clergy. She said, "No" but knew who I was seeing. It was Christ – not Jesus – but Christ. She went on to explain that there are three different Christs, one who expressed himself as Jesus and another who never came into human form. He stayed love and light directly from source. My client did also remember a past life in the clergy. We did not talk about the third Christ.

I found this intriguing and wanted to ask you about it. Is what I saw true? Is her explanation true?

R: Yes, it is true, but perhaps a bit different than what you both experienced. We all come from source, that much is true. When we split off from source, we express ourselves in different ways. Some inhabit bodies. Some of those bodies are human. Some are aliens, some are animals, some are other creatures that you don't yet know exist. Some souls break away but do not go into a body. They remain love and light. When they interact with other souls, they can alter the way they communicate or appear in ways which are easier or more palatable to the soul. In your case, this soul of love and light looked like a Christ.

R: In your client's case she had previous experience with this soul and was able to immediately make the connection between what you saw and her former communication with this soul.

As far as the name Christ, look around you on planet Earth. There are multiple Bobs, Michaels, Catherines, and even versions of your name, Kristi, which is inspired by the name Christ. There are even many Jesuses. Although when you think of Jesus, you think of the son of God and not the Jesus down the street.

Here's where people get confused. They are all children of God. Whether the name is Christ, Bob, Jesus, or Barbara. We all come from source and are therefore all extensions of source. So, it would make perfect sense that there are multiple Christs. There are certainly multiple versions of the name Christ.

K: So how are all these Christs different from each other?

R: How is anybody different from everybody else? The Christs came to Earth in human form with different things to learn and experience. The Christ the two of you experienced showed itself as we all are – love and light – and not the fallible human interpretation of love and light.

K: Thank you for that clarification. My head is now bent and twisted.

R: This explanation is a way for you to understand in a way that the human brain can comprehend. There is so much more which is beyond human comprehension. We will divulge that information as you, the human race, evolves and has the capacity to understand.

K: I can hardly wait! So why did this Christ energy show up yesterday? Was it part of my client's reading? My reading? Or just a fluke?

R: A fluke? Really? Oh, that's funny! It was a mutual learning experience for the two of you. Yes, it was part of your client's evolution, but as you know when we deliver messages and information it can show up in a myriad of ways. Yesterday, your lesson showed up with the love and light energy of a Christ but through your client. Surprise!

K: Yes, it was a surprise, but a good surprise and I thank you.

R: You are most welcome, dear one.

February 31, 2022

K: I'm noticing I'm getting a bit more worn out working with people lately. Why is that? Is it my age? Am I taking on too much? Has the energy of the people I see shifted or is it something else?

R: It is mostly what you've listed above. The biggest factor is how people are reacting to the pandemic. The tension is building. People can only go along for so long without exploding or imploding. You're seeing both. Add that to your own frustrations and it will certainly affect your energy. As always, work on yourself first. What are your dreams? Your frustrations? When you work on you, it becomes easier to spot those same things in others and guide them through it. Right now, you're frustrated because they need guidance, but so do you. You want your clients to have the motivation and belief that they deserve to be happy. It's a beautiful thing to see when it happens, isn't it?

K: It's my favorite. In my effort to help people recognize their true beauty, it's the ones who believe that it is true and possible that make my heart sing. It's taken me years to thrive in my own life. For those who are ready, I'm the person, or rather one of the people, who can help. All they have to do is say yes.

R: Yes, but only when they are ready to say yes. Don't dump too much stuff on them at once or the magic will be lost. Be content with the timing of the messages you deliver and then be content with the way it is received. Do we need to remind you that everyone is different? Be gentle with yourself and others. You can expect and wish the world for them, but don't be disappointed if they don't want that for themselves.

You want to help everybody. What you're forgetting is that people hear, see, and learn in different ways and in different timeframes. You talk about people coming to you and wanting an instant "fix" and yet you are expecting the same thing out of yourself. You want instant fixes for them, too. Slow and steady wins the race, my dear.

Also, not everyone is going to resonate with you. That's why there are so many other healers. People will resonate with different healers and in different ways. That's why we connect to so many people, too. The message is the same, but the messengers are very different simply because people are different.

March 6. 2022

K: I have a couple of questions for you.

R: Yes? Go ahead.

K: Is there a name for the collective which you are the voice of?

R: It is the Ramadear Collective.

K: Really? I know of a few other psychics that channel the RA. What's the difference?

R: Many people channel different collectives. There are thousands of collectives. Each person who channels the RA, or any other collective, connects with a different energy within that collective depending on what they are here to channel. Some energies in a collective represent politics. Others represent climate change. Others speak about humanity.

It's like the human race goes to school, which it does, and goes from class-to-class learning from different teachers on different subjects. The voices of the collective are those teachers. Think about when you were in school. Some students slept through class; some were there because they had to be. Others were fascinated and paid rapt attention. This all varied depending on the student's connection to the subject and the teacher. In fact, it even depended on the connection to school and to life itself. Can you now see the comparison to these collectives? Also, some students, while in school, excelled at science. Others in math, still others in the arts. The voices of the collectives will connect with humans who already have a talent in a particular subject and then communicate new information to them in an effort to help the planet evolve. Because you live on a planet of free will, it is still up to the recipient on how they choose to use that information. Can you now see the comparison to school and to life itself?

K: Yes, I can, thank you.

May 10, 2022

K: I, along with the rest of the world, need some major guidance. We are in such a state right now. People are coming unglued. We still have the pandemic. There is a war in Europe going on. Inflation is at a high point. Roe v. Wade is being overturned after 50 years. All this combined with the usual craziness of violence is making so many people want to give up or fight even harder. I have to agree with many. These are unprecedented times which seem to bring even more madness to the world, if that's possible. What can we do about it? How can I be a voice of reason when many times I feel like I'm losing my sanity too?

R: What's happening is that your world is hitting rock bottom. You can equate it to an alcoholic or drug addict or what you like to refer to as the cast iron life preserver. People are fighting for their lives and are in complete denial of what's really going on. They, the people on your planet, are killing themselves but think they are doing things that are healthy. Is fighting healthy? Never. Standing up for yourself is healthy, but fighting is not. Is listening to the news that is nothing but "if it bleeds it leads" healthy? Never. You listen to the news because you've been shamed into thinking that you need to know what's going on in the world around you. Believe us, all you have to do is open your front door and you'll know what's going on around you.

Your planet needs an intervention. Just like any addictive behavior, you need outside help – an intervention.

K: Who is going to do the intervention? Are you talking about extraterrestrials?

R: Exactly. That's another reason so many people are having extraterrestrial and paranormal experiences; to wake them up. Because your planet is a planet of free will there is only so much extraterrestrials can do. The same is true of any intervention plan. The addict is sent to a rehab facility, but it is always their choice whether to stay or go. Even if they stay for the entire recovery time they can still leave and immediately start drinking or using again. You see? Free will.

Your planet is exactly like any addict in the world. You think you know what is best. You don't. Your politicians and corporations are your drug dealers. You want more and more of what they have to offer even though you know it's bad for you. You continue on with this behavior because it gives you some kind of high. You're beginning to realize that the high is temporary, so you keep going back to your dealers for more and more of the same drug.

Because you live on a free will planet, extraterrestrials can help but cannot interfere – much like any addiction counselor. You can acknowledge what they say and are trying to do, or you can run and hide. You can also make fun of and ridicule those who have had contact to make yourself feel better. Much like addicts who judge others who don't use as being "square" or whatever label is trending at the time.

Your planet needs to pay attention to those who are trying to help. Yes, those are the extraterrestrials but also those who are listening to the messages from the other side. There are still millions of you with a voice of reason. They are the teachers for the rest of the world. The world only needs to listen! It all is really so simple. You just need to listen.

R: I already know your next question.

K: I'm sure you do.

R: Who exactly are we supposed to listen to? That is your question, correct?

K: Yes, that is my question.

R: Quit listening to your politicians! Quit listening to your corporations! Quit listening to your news stations! They all have an agenda. Their agenda is more profits, more viewers, more money. They all claim to care about you and whatever country you reside in but once in position, the pressure to win is insurmountable. That's why politicians sign certain bills which they think will help their constituents, but slithered inside that particular bill is a bunch of other smaller changes which harm you and your planet. Your politicians sign certain bills thinking that no one will even pay attention to the small stuff (which is true) and will only pay attention to the main point of the bill, which makes them a hero in their own state or country.

Just like healing is done in baby steps, hurting and decline is done in baby steps too. Do you think that the woes you mentioned earlier are new? Absolutely not. All of this has been in the making for generations. Baby step by baby step until now, it feels like you are drowning in a sea of chaotic neurosis. It's true. You are drowning. Just like the addict – they don't begin using every day. They begin typically with pressure from family or friends. Every day, week, month, or year, they need more and more of what is perceived as happiness to feel even normal. That's exactly what is happening to your planet. They need more and more of what is perceived as freedom, independence, and happiness when all it's doing is making you more and more of an addict – more and more unhappy.

So, what can you do about it? Listen to your heart. Listen to your souls. Connect and listen to your guides. How do you do that? Most of you are so disconnected you don't even know how to listen to your heart, your soul, or how to connect to your guides. Begin by paying attention. Do something nice for someone else. Since we really are all one, doing something nice for someone else really is doing something nice for yourself. Isn't that a great way to begin? Then, you reach out to professionals who really do understand the chaos we are in as a planet.

Listen, pay attention, and do the work they recommend that you do. This will get you started. You can invest money and time working with certain healers or you can begin by searching You Tube! That is free! Read a book recommended by healers. You can buy books, or you can go to your local library and borrow books for free! There really is no excuse. Help is out there. Cost is just another excuse.

Think again of your addicts. They spend thousands of dollars each week to keep themselves addicted. You don't have to do that. Make a commitment to yourself to heal. Then, you too can be a voice of reason in your crazy, but beautiful world. Understand that awakening to a healthy you and a healthy planet is done in baby steps. You will fall, you will falter, but you pick yourself up and try again. Just keep going. Do not give up on yourself and don't give up on mankind. Just like any addict, once they commit to a sober life, they surround themselves with people who are healthy for them. They go to meetings; they go to other healers. They do whatever it takes to keep themselves sober and healthy. There isn't a long-term addict in recovery that wants to go back to the life of an addict. Once they've learned to escape that life, they understand how unhealthy it really was. It is a much easier life to be clean and sober. The life of an addict is hard – unbearably hard. The same is true of the way many people on your planet are living today. Once you commit to a healthy life and stick with it, you too will understand how much easier life is when you don't buy into the lies and manipulation of those supposedly in power. No. You are the one in power! Understand that and embrace it and start living it!

May 17, 2022

K: I live a peaceful and quiet life, which I love. I also love the work that I do. I'm so happy clients are reaching out to me for guidance, but it does get incredibly heavy sometimes trying to get people to heal and live their best lives. How can I still enjoy my work and not be affected negatively by others' energy? After all, they are reaching out for help.

R: How long did it take you to change your life?

K: Decades. I guess if we're talking years, it would be about 45 years. Ok, I understand. People grow and change at their own rate. I guess where I really want to go with this is just when people are ready to change, it seems something else tragic is happening in the world today and keeping people in grief.

R: That much is true. That is why we are writing this book. Sometimes it takes tragedy after tragedy for people to hit rock bottom; for them to decide they don't want to live like they have been living anymore. Again, we're back on the topic of addiction. The biggest addiction in the world is the addiction to suffering. When people begin to realize that they don't have to suffer even when there is unspeakable tragedy happening all around them, that is when the real healing begins.

It doesn't mean people shouldn't care. It doesn't mean that they shouldn't help others in need. But what it does mean is that you have chosen to attend a play of Greek tragedy proportions. It is a play. Nothing about your life or any life around you is real. When you can understand that, you can participate to the level you choose, but you don't have to give up your life or suffer through its entirety.

Work inside yourself. Why did you pick this time in history to come to your planet? What lessons are you supposed to be learning from your experiences here? How can you be of assistance to others who don't understand life at the level you do? Be strong in who you are and why you are here. Understand that pain creates pain. Many souls on your planet get their worth from surviving. How many get their worth from thriving? How many get their worth from simply existing? The fact that you exist is enough. If you add in service to others all the better. How can you be of service to others? Is everyone happy, grateful, and thriving today? No? Then there is work to be done. How can you be of service to others to change that?

That's why your planet is so difficult. It IS filled with tragedy. Who is going to step up and help? Who is going to stay strong and focused through it all? Or who is going to create more chaos? Who is going to hurt others? Those are vital roles which are being played too. The so-called villain plays a vital role in your society. They can be the teacher just as much as the healer. Most souls on your planet just haven't realized that yet. They won't realize it either until it is their time to transition, and everything is made clear on the other side. They will reincarnate time and time again until they do understand the part they came to play, as well as the part the others came to play. Yes, there are good guys and bad guys, but on the other side they are simply souls playing a part in their own evolution as well as helping you in your evolution.

K: I understand much of what you're saying, but how do you reconcile some of the acts of pure evil going on right now? When a woman is raped? When a man is tortured? When one man is carrying out genocide on an entire county?

R: We agree with you. All the things you mention are horrible. That's why living a life on your planet is so difficult. The things that happen on planet Earth would never happen anywhere else in the galaxy. You all have subjected yourself to unspeakable experiences. Even those of you who are on Earth living a relatively easy life are considered heroic by any other planet's standards.

K: So why do we do it? Why did we come here? I have a hard time believing that volunteering to come to a planet to experience the unspeakable is something we'd — anyone — would volunteer to do. Yes, I know it is for the soul to evolve, but I need a better explanation than that. I need to know why the soul needs to evolve and why it has to suffer to evolve. This is what is overwhelming to me today. I need another level of understanding.

August 2, 2022

K: Good Morning. I'm so sorry we didn't get to finish our last conversation. I needed a break but didn't anticipate it would be a 2.5-month break.

R: That's fine. We've still been communicating but not in the original way of automatic writing. Are you ready to pick up where we left off?

K: Not quite. I had a reading from a wonderful lady across the country who also channels from a collective. She gave me some things to ponder that I would now like to ask you. I would like a little more background information from you if that is alright with you.

R: Please proceed.

K: From which density do you come from?

R: I am from the 6th density getting ready to ascend to 7th density. Our work together is helping that ascension.

K: You mentioned earlier that you are from the RA collective, but in the reading I was told that you are actually from the Ramadear collective. Which is true?

R: They both are true. As I mentioned to you the collective is made up of many different voices all seeking to ascend. The Ramadear collective is a smaller group of voices/spirits from the RA collective. You will be correct naming both collectives but going forward, if you feel more comfortable, please state we are from the Ramadear collective.

K: Thank you, I will. Am I correct in assuming that the Ramadear collective teaches the Law of One?

R: You are correct. That is why we are communicating with you. The original Law of One is difficult for many to read and understand. The different voices in the Ramadear collective are reaching out to many different humans to interpret the teachings in a more modern way, so more people can have a better understanding of what the Law of One actually is. We will go into that in greater detail later.

K: OK, thank you. So, tell me, what is your background? You said you hail from Eurates, but where is that? Have you ever been human? Even though you are 6th density, how do I know you are speaking the truth? How do I know you have the highest good of our planet as your mission?

R: These are good questions. Yes, I am from Eurates which is in the Andromedin star system. These are your origins too, which is one of the reasons we picked you to communicate through. We are a telepathic collective and we need someone to take our telepathic messages and translate them into the English language. That person is you.

K: Yikes. Not too much responsibility!

R: We trust you and we believe in you.

K: Is collaborating on this project with you helping my soul's growth too?

R: Of course. You have already ascended to 4th density. By accepting this project, you will be taking the next steps in your soul's growth.

K: OK, that should be inspiration enough for me to continue.

R: We hope so and believe in you.

K: Thank you. I'm not saying I won't let you down, but I will certainly try not to. I think I'm ready to pick up where we left off in May. Why do we choose to come to planet Earth? Why do we do unspeakable things to each other? Why do we choose to experience some of the horrors that exist?

R: You asked for another level of understanding, correct? Here it is. It comes down to the Law of One. Souls incarnate for two different reasons: the first is for their soul to evolve. The soul does this by setting themselves up for certain lessons, things they want to learn, accomplish, and experience which are only available on Earth. As you are now somewhat familiar with the Law of One and have learned, we all come to be of service to others or be of service to self. When we are of service to others our soul will evolve or ascend. Service to others means the soul now knows we are all one. We all originate from source. What you do to or for others, you do to or for yourself.

Those that are here for service to self are not helping themselves, others, or even the planet to evolve or ascend. They only see things as separate. Until they learn and truly understand that we are all one, they will have to keep coming back and coming back until they do learn that simple but massive lesson. The horrendous crimes that you see are typically souls who are so disconnected from source and are in service to self. Most of these souls will live out their lives in service to self – others might eventually connect with source and realize the atrocities they've done to others.

The other reason some souls come to Earth is to help raise the vibration of the planet. These souls are called Starseeds. In essence, we are all Starseeds because we are or were all seeded from other planets or star systems. But those who have had more lives off planet Earth than on planet Earth are considered Starseeds. As we discussed earlier with the influx of people on your planet, many are what we call newer souls. They too have had fewer human lives but are at the beginning stages of learning the main lesson that we are all one. Starseeds also have had fewer Earth lives, but they have learned the lessons, or they come here knowing we are all one and understand they need to balance the energy of the "new" human souls.

I hope this helps you understand why souls choose to come to Earth. There really are many, many reasons, but it boils down to two main reasons. Also, one of the worst "crimes" is to destroy a planet. That is exactly what is happening to your planet which is also why so many Starseeds are arriving or waking up to their true purpose – to save your planet from yourselves.

K: So, I've always believed and taught that there is no right or wrong. There is only what is right or wrong for you and only you know the answer to that. Is that true or not?

R: It is true to a point. In your life path, you may have agreed to be the "bad guy" this time around to help another soul or group of souls to achieve their life lessons. There is no wrong with that. People make very interesting choices in their life journeys. Does it mean some of the choices are wrong? Typically, no. It brings them where they are today so how could that be wrong? Making perceived bad choices might be the catalyst to help them decide what they don't want and what no longer serves them.

As we've discussed before, you can't judge anyone for you know not the path they've chosen to walk in this lifetime. Where wrong comes into play is in the destruction of your planet. You can destroy your own home, but you cannot destroy the home of billions of other people. That's where we have the right to interfere and believe me, we are getting perilously close to interfering. Supply and demand seem to rule the day and with demand at such a high, supply from natural resources will become extinct very soon. This means starvation for the people of Earth, as Earth is already beginning to starve. This can lead to the eventual destruction of the planet as a whole.

Is this what you want for your world? To have no world? So, destruction of your planet is the only wrong that we see from our vantage point.

K: Thank you. What can we do as a people to keep this from happening?

R: There are many things you can do. We will list a few here for you to begin.

    a. Grow your own food – pesticide free
    b. Quit eating processed food – it is killing you.
    c. When you grow your own food and quit eating processed food, there is little to no waste to litter your planet. Recycling is a great start but barely makes a dent in your waste. So, become conscious of the packaging you throw away.
    d. Start practicing precycling. Buy things in biodegradable packaging.
    e. This is very controversial, but control your population growth. This should be done as a conscious choice and not a government mandate. The more people on your planet the more is consumed, and more waste is produced.
    f. Support unity with each other! Understand that all are here for different reasons and shouldn't be judged for being who they are. If someone, however, harms another person there are consequences. The divisiveness you now experience does all harm and no good for the people and the planet.

g. Have the courage to be yourself! That's where so much pain and harm come from; people are trying to be what they think others expect of them. It always ends in disaster. Today, begin the path to creating who you are – who you came here to be. That is the path to happiness for yourself and others.

We think these seven things are a great beginning to the saving of your planet. There are millions of other ways, but these are great ways to begin. Bless you all on your journey.

August 8, 2022

K: How do people save themselves?

R: If people begin by saving themselves, they will automatically be saving the planet. When people love themselves, they save themselves. They can't help but love others, and that includes their own home, for your Earth home most certainly has a soul and is a living, breathing thing.

K: So how do people begin to love themselves?

R: Intent is everything. First, people must want to love themselves. This happens in small every minute of everyday decisions. Quit treating yourselves like you don't deserve happiness! Look outside of yourself for just a minute; do you want your family and friends to be happy? Most people will answer "yes" to this question. If you want your family and friends to be happy, you must first start with yourself. This is not said as a way to promote selfish, narcissistic behavior. When you do things to make yourself happy, you lead by example. You then give your family and friends permission to do the same thing! You teach and give to others by giving to yourself first!

So many people think they must sacrifice for others to be happy. That is simply not true. When parents, in particular, are vocal about the sacrifices they made for their children, what ultimately can happen is that the children grow up with guilt or entitlement, neither one being healthy.

Parents need to teach their children how to be aware of the world around them. If they are privileged, go with them to volunteer to help those who are not privileged. Show them how important it is to help others. Help them feel the sense of oneness when you care for others.

For parents who struggle, show your children that the cycle doesn't need to continue. Begin working with your children at a very young age. Ask them questions, such as what makes you happy? What makes your heart sing? Even if that child doesn't know or even just shrugs their shoulders in apathy or defiance, know that you are planting seeds of thought for them. We have been programmed from a very young age to not be happy. Did you know that? We are programmed not to be happy – that we should be content with whatever life hands to us. With a spiritual journey we KNOW we are meant to be happy. It is our natural state of being.

Society fools us into thinking that happiness is outside of ourselves. The house, the car, the right friends, and connections. No one tells us that the key to true happiness is right inside of ourselves. We just need to take the time, sit in silence, and ask ourselves the same questions; what makes me happy? What makes my heart sing? When you have the answers, start asking your friends, your family, your loved ones those exact same questions. When people focus on their own happiness it is contagious. Others will begin to look at them too for guidance, inspiration, and advice. Happiness is now an epidemic! Happy people take care of themselves, others, and their home. It doesn't matter how much or how little you have, happiness can be there at any age, any income level, any city, any country, any gender, any ethnicity. In other words, anybody and everybody deserves to be happy.

This is how people learn to love themselves. Make yourself happy first. Love for others comes naturally after that.

August 10, 2022

K: Speaking of happiness – some people I've worked with claim never to have known happiness. How can that be? Depression seems to be an epidemic in this country too, and the answer seems to be medication. I've got nothing against medication. I think Western medicine is needed, but the answer always seems to be to throw a pill at it. We've got a nation, if not a world that is completely medicated. Can you explain this to me?

R: It is true. You live in a world of medicated people. Medicated parents are raising children, so they naturally gravitate to medication, too. Your world has become very disconnected with each other. It used to be that you would meet up with friends, family, co-workers, etc. With the creation of smart phones, with the world basically at your fingertips, the need for human heart-to-heart contact is being replaced by electronics to electronics contact. The coronavirus exacerbated this where electronic contact was all that was available. It was a "life saver" in many people's existence. It did serve a purpose, and it still does, but what is missing is heart-to-heart contact.

People think they are connecting through electronic devices, your television is included in this, but it is a very shallow and superficial way of connecting. It was fun for a while but now people are experiencing the effects of relationships which aren't heart-centered.

You've heard stories of children raised in orphanages? They were deprived of touch, of daily contact with others except for other children who were experiencing the same thing. It got to the point where many of them didn't or couldn't recover even when adopted. Humans are pack animals and are designed to need each other. What is happening with electronic devices is similar, albeit in a slower fashion, to children raised in certain orphanages. If things don't change – if you don't return to heart-centered communication your societies will have taken one more step towards being completely controlled by forces outside themselves. This has been in the works for years.

Like many things, inventions are meant to make your lives easier and more convenient. But as with all opposing forces, there is a dark side to most every invention. That dark side is now becoming obvious to those who are willing to see the truth.

August 15, 2022

K: Why do so many people live as victims?

R: It is where they are comfortable. It gives them the attention they didn't get in a healthy way when they were young, so they become satisfied with unhealthy attention as they grow older. Then, it becomes routine until they are completely stuck and can't see a way out, even though they really don't want to find a way out.

K: I find that victims carry so much anger. Do you find that to be true?

R: Absolutely. They are angry because they see themselves as victims and nobody comes to rescue them. Therefore, there is someone else to blame other than themselves. They put themselves in a perceived helpless position which then gives them the right to be angry. The thing is when someone does try to help them, they become resentful. How dare you try to help me! There is nothing wrong with me! There is only something wrong with you! In other words, there are always excuses and blame to keep them stuck and keep them the victim. They are then justified in their behavior.

K: Crazy how some people are so unaware of their own behaviors.

R: Are you including yourself in that category?

K: Well, crap, I guess so. May I say I've been working very hard at understanding myself.

R: We know that, and you've made tremendous progress. We are very proud of you and the work that you do. We also love to tease.

K: Ha Ha. Very funny, but true.

K: I'm also feeling a bit disconnected from friends that I've had for many, many years. Their opinions and views on life I'm finding very disconcerting. Why is that?

R: You all are changing, but in different ways. What you once had in common really no longer exists. They are learning their lessons, just as you are learning yours. Those lessons are just different now for each of you.

K: I'm trying to incorporate what I'm learning from The Law of One which is being in service to others on this planet. Sometimes it just feels so vibrationally dissonant from where I'm going and what I'm doing compared to other's path. I'm at the point of do I even want to be around certain people anymore? All people have great qualities which I love, but there are other qualities which hurt my soul. I'm just not sure how to handle it. Can you offer some guidance?

R: You are a planet of free will. You can handle it however you choose. If something no longer serves your growth, it's time to walk away. If there is something that continues to serve your highest good, stay with it.

K: Obviously, there is something there that continues to serve my highest good or I would have walked away a long time ago. I'll trust my intuition if or when it's time to walk away.

R: Good decision. It's always best to trust your intuition and remember not everyone is here for the same reason you are. The people you walk away from could be your best teachers. But then again, maybe not. Maybe it's time to graduate to another level.

August 28, 2022

K: Thanks for your patience. For some reason I haven't felt very connected to you and writing. I've now made another commitment to write every day until I leave for vacation.

R: Commitments are good as long as they are goals and guilt isn't attached to breaking that goal.

K: I usually don't carry much guilt, but I do feel bad when I don't write for a period of time.

R: No worries, Let's carry on.

K: First, thank you for the questions you gave to me during my morning coffee. I think that part of the reason for not writing is that I'm not sure where to go with questions, so I thank you for the inspiration this morning. How do you and the rest of the collective fit in with what we humans understand as God?

R: As you know, we are all one which means I, the collective, you, and all of humanity are pieces of divinity. We are all God, just expressing ourselves in different ways.

K: I do understand that, but it is also my understanding that ego is what makes humans different from each other. Ego temporarily separates us so we can experience different things while in human form.

R: That is correct.

K: It is also my understanding that once we return to spirit there is no more ego.

R: That is also correct.

K: So how can you be in spirit, have no ego, yet be separate from God?

R: I am not separate from God, and neither are you. I, along with the rest of the collective, are just vibrating at a higher level than you and most humans. God is infinite but vibrates at different levels within that infinity. I, and the collective, vibrate at 6th density. You are vibrating at 4th density which is one of the reasons you can hear us in the collective. Most humans vibrate at 3rd density and therefore cannot receive the communications we send out.

We are there for anyone who wants to communicate with us. Most people don't want to. They are busy surviving and can't see anything else beyond that. You and other humans who are vibrating at a higher density can then communicate with those at a higher density if they choose. Remember when we first connected?

K; Yes, very well!

R: You put pen to paper and asked to connect to spirit operating at a high vibration. We heard you and answered your call. Actually, we have been waiting for you to "show up" for many years. You just didn't know you could connect with us and didn't really know how. You stopped at connecting with your guides. Which, by the way, is a great place to start. Most people just don't understand there is more. There are an infinite number of possibilities and ways to connect with spirit, but your vibration needs to be able to match spirit's vibration to a certain degree. You've noticed in the past several years that you've had bouts of vertigo?

K: Yes, I have.

R: That is what it feels like to ascend to 4th density.

K: Yeah, well, not very fun.

R: You asked, and we answered. If you were eating better the symptoms of ascension would have been milder.

K: Now that I'm at 4th density, do I still need to eat lighter?

R: Only if you want to continue to ascend. Also, it will help you in your psychic medium business if you alter what you eat.

K: Well, crap. I love food.

R: Yes, we know. (Said with love and laughter) You can still eat what you love, just eat less of it, and change your portions. Less meat and more vegetables.

K: Yeah, yeah, I can do that. Just don't expect a miracle.

R: Too late, you are already a miracle.

K: Ah, that's very sweet.

R: Don't take it too personally. Everyone is a miracle. Most people just don't know it. You are just now beginning to understand the miracle of human existence or the fact that you do exist at all.

K: You giveth and you taketh away.

R: We say the words. You do the interpreting of their meaning.

K: It always falls back on me, doesn't it?

R: Always has and always will. Because when it falls back on you, it falls back on all of us. The Law of One.

K: So, does this human cycle ever end? Do we ever all go back to source?

R: Everything is cyclical. So, humankind might end at some time, but energy merely changes form. So, the personality known as Kristi will end/die, but the spirit/soul that is Kristi will just change form into something else which might include surrendering and going back to source now vibrating at a much higher level. Your goal, even though you are not aware of it at this time is to leave the human form and be part of a collective, too – just as I am.

K: What?!

R: Don't worry that is a long way off. You have not earned your wings as yet.

K: Yeah, if I had wings, they'd be tarnished.

R: You can say that again.

You are in the beginning stages of this goal. You've had many lifetimes as a healer. This life combines many of the gifts of those other lifetimes. When you completely come from a place of love, you have ascended to 6th density and will be able to vibrate harmoniously with other members of a collective. But you will not be able to reach 6th density while in human form. You will also have to do soul work in between other incarnations. Now, it's my turn to ask you a question.

K: Oh, God. OK.

R: Does everything you think say and do come from a place of love?

K: I think you already know the answer to that.

R: Yes, we do, that is one of the reasons we are with you now; to help you understand where you are today and where you need to be in the future.

K: I've got a long way to go in the love department, although I certainly have made some strides in this lifetime. Every time I think I'm making progress, you throw a wrench into my loving intent, and it quickly gets replaced with frustration, judgement, or anger.

R: Exactly. When you get to the point of never being triggered by other people or situations outside yourself, you will be ready to move on.

K: It feels like everything is outside of us, yet everything is inside ourselves.

R: You've got it! In human existence, programming is to make you look outside yourself. Really, you should observe outside yourself but know that nothing really exists that isn't inside yourself. You created it and you can alter it. You have the power in you to create anything you want. Most people don't understand this, and they give their power away to the lowest bidder.

K: Ouch. That hurt. I understand it, but am disheartened by how long it's taken me to reach out and ask the questions; to want more joy for myself and everyone.

R: Even if you were able to give joy to everyone, many would turn it down. There is a certain satisfaction in living in misery. Many people think that is how life is supposed to be lived. Trust us, it's not. Yes, you are in human form to learn lessons, accomplish things, and experience things. Everyone does that – no exception but many people think that it needs to be hard. It doesn't. Even many spiritual teachers tell us that the lessons are hard. It's only because their lessons have been hard. It truly doesn't have to be that way.

K: Wow, even I teach that sometimes.

R: We know. It's not that you're doing it wrong, because typically you are working with people who have lived as if it's hard. You are trying to undo some of that damage which can be painful. Just start paying attention to what you say and how you say it. Start telling people that it truly doesn't have to be hard! Find joy and laughter in the unwinding of previous programming. We'd like to add a caveat to this; life can be and is hard, but humans make it much harder than it really needs to be.

K: Amazing. I will start paying better attention to that. Thank you so much,

R: Blessings to you, dear one.

August 29, 2022

K: How can I best be of service to others in the time I have left on this planet?

R: Since you live on a planet of free will, there is nothing you have to do. You can just retire and live life as you choose.

K: Yes, I do know that but I'm not ready for that just yet. I want to continue to be of service to this planet and am asking for guidance on what is needed most that also fits my skill set.

R: You are doing a beautiful job just by being you. The people who can benefit most from what you have to say are finding their way to you. Are you looking for something additional to do?

K: Yes, if it would benefit humankind. I really want to get on large stages, so I can reach more people. Is that a possibility?

R: Yes, it is a possibility. Are you sure this is something you want to do?

K: Yes, I'm sure. I want it to happen before I'm too freaking old!

R: Your speaking will begin to improve and grow when this book has been released.

K: That's still a way off.

R: Yes, but everything is within divine timing.

K: Ok, I'll trust you, but this body isn't getting any younger.

R: Think about it this way. Even after you make your transition, you can help people through the books you've written. They are your legacy. Look at the impact the collective is having on you, and we are not in human form.

K: That's true, maybe my legacy can be my books or maybe I can come through in spirit to those who are willing to connect.

R: True. As you know, with so many Starseeds awakening on Earth, telepathy is becoming more common and easier for those who are willing to listen, to tap into, and to ask questions of those on the other side of the veil.

K: True. But it feels achingly slow to get people to understand.

R: It has taken millennia for humans to get to where they are today. You can't expect them to change overnight. Actually, that's when much of the change does happen – overnight! While people are sleeping and connecting to their guides that way.

K: Ha! Very funny. Yes, change can happen overnight, but in many overnights. That's how much of my change has happened; by listening to my dreams, paying attention to messages from my guides. When I was ready, I started changing during the daylight hours, too.

R: That's how it happens. There is ancestral trauma that affects the DNA of each subsequent generation. It is a conscious choice of each individual to continue or to break the cycle. That commitment is a lifetime commitment, and many people think it's too hard, so they quit after a short time or don't even try to begin with it.

K: It's my understanding that ETs are also altering our DNA. Is it for the same purpose? Or are they creating hybrid races or are they helping to heal ancestral trauma?

R: They are not healing ancestral trauma. That is up to each individual and their life plan when they come into human form. ETs are altering the DNA of only the people with whom they have contact and not even all of those.

K: I know my DNA has been altered and I know it's not for birthing children since I don't have any. So why have they altered mine?

R: Your DNA has been altered for the children you DO have but are considered hybrids. By altering your DNA, the children produced on crafts are coming closer to being able to inhabit Earth without looking unusual. In other words, they can better blend in. The children produced before the DNA alterations were able to sustain life, but look very alien and don't resemble humans. As far as producing children, your days of that kind of involvement are through. Your participation is greatly appreciated.

K: OK, my DNA has been altered. Since my "breeding" days are over, will the ETs again alter my DNA back to the way it was before children?

R: The DNA altering is multi-layered. The other reason for the DNA changes is to help you with your service on the Galactic Federation of Planets.

K: I know I serve on that council but how is it different now that my DNA has been altered?

R: You were unable to attend many meetings because of the change in atmospheric energy. In the meetings, you were able to attend you couldn't stay for long because the energy shift would affect your human body upon return to Earth.

K: Wow, crazy. Is that also why many times I feel dizzy upon awakening? Or do I just feel tired like I've had little to no sleep?

R: Precisely. You should have also noticed that those symptoms have greatly reduced in the past year or so.

K: Yes, I have noticed.

R: That is due to the DNA changes made within you. You are now better able to cope with your spirit leaving your human body to attend to galactic issues. Now do you also see when you ask if there is something else you can do to be of service to humankind, we tell you that you are already doing it?

K: Ah yeah, I guess so. Crazy.

R: Not so crazy when you know and see the bigger picture. You are being of service to not only humans and planet Earth, but you are also being of service to many other planets and many other races of beings on those planets.

K: That's quite a lot to take in today. I knew much of this information, such as being on the council of the Galactic Federation of Planets, but I didn't know that was also part of the DNA changes.

R: Now you know. If you would have been privy to this information even a few years ago you would have poo-poo'd it thinking you'd made it all up, correct?

K: Yes, very correct. I still question it. Am I still making it all up? Am I crazy?

R: On one level you are making it all up. Everyone is. Remember you create your own reality, just like everybody else. The difference is you are making it all up while in human form and living on planet Earth. Once your spirit leaves your body, everything will become abundantly clear. It will feel absolutely normal that you serve on this council and that you have hybrid children. It's the human part of you that has trouble accepting it because it goes against everything you've ever been taught. You CAN be in two places at the same time. You can be in your bed asleep and yet your spirit can be working for the galactic greater good. There is additional detail to follow but for today, this is enough for you to wrap your human head around. Blessing to you always.

August 30, 2022

K: That was a great session yesterday, thank you.

R: You are most welcome.

K: How long have I been on the council of the Galactic Federation of Planets?

R: 500

K: 500 what? Years? Incarnations? Days? I'd like a bit more clarity please.

R: We don't measure things in years, incarnations, or days. 500 is the best we can give you at this time.

K: Well, ok. I guess it really doesn't matter how long. It still blows me away that I'm on the council at all. What is my main responsibility?

R: To listen to input from every race from every planet represented. The goal of the council is peace, understanding, communication, and inclusion.

K: Sounds like what Earth is attempting to do, and not always successfully. Are there planets which are not included? If so, why?

R: There are many planets which are not included. Some because they have no form of life. Others because they don't care to be represented, and others because their goals run counter to those of the council's goals.

K: If my main goal is to listen, what then? Do I just listen, or do I take what I hear and take action in any way?

R: As you know you are what you refer to as a galactic first responder. As you interact with beings from planets needing help from the council. You are able to understand their needs on a level not understood by others. You handle the work on a planet in need with diplomacy and in accordance with the laws of that planet.

K: I wish I had those same skills here on Earth! Impatience seems to rule my behavior here.

R: You are correct, and we find the dichotomy humorous.

K: Yeah, well, I find this whole thing humorous. I mean who is even going to believe some of this stuff that we're discussing?

R: Those who need to hear what we have to say will resonate with the words and grow from them and then tell others.

K: I'm trusting you, as I trust my guides.

R: Good. As people open more and more, they will be ready for additional details of what life really means and what else exists besides the 3D world. People are hungry for more information that they can embrace, understand, and incorporate into their daily lives.

September 1, 2022

K: What is the best way for others to be of service to others?

R: To simply be themselves. The trouble is that very few people truly know who they are. To the readers of this book, begin by understanding yourself, not the you that you created to please others. Your time is now. What makes your heart sing? What makes time fly? What fills that void in your solar plexus? That's where you begin. You all came to this planet with certain gifts. It's never too late to claim them and awaken them. When you figure out what makes your heart sing, we guarantee you will be in service to others. They go hand in hand.

You don't have to be of service to others in the same way that your friends or family are. You came here to be unique, and the world needs you and your talents, your gifts. Trust that it is enough. Your social media allows others to judge. Pay no attention. The only thing you need to pay attention to is what makes you happy without hurting others. You don't need to save the whole world – just your small corner of it. Just think, if everybody did what made them happy, the world would be in a much better place.

The leaders of countries on your planet think they know what is best for you, their country, and the planet as a whole. Trust me – they don't. Only YOU know what is best for you. It just takes diligence and commitment to yourself to figure that out.

So how do you really begin? Pay attention to that niggling thought in the back of your head. You know; the thought you buried a long time ago. The thought that started with – wouldn't that be fun? Or I'd like to try that. Usually, the minute you have those thoughts you shove them deep inside of yourself for fear of judgement from yourself or from others. You think it couldn't possibly happen to you. You're not good enough. You're not smart enough. What if you fail? Sound familiar? Feel familiar?

So, my question to you is, "So what?" Trust that you probably will fail, be terrible at, or the odds are stacked against you. So what? You'll never know unless you try. And try again. And try again until you are no longer bad at something. You are now good at something! Eventually, you will be great at something. Exhume those negative and judging thoughts. Bring them to life then release them! Find out what makes you happy! The painter makes the purchaser happy because of the joy put into the work of the painting. The musician makes the listener happy because of the joy of composing, singing, and playing the instrument.

The accountant, the one who loves math, makes the boss happy because now all have a clear picture of finances. The garbage collector, who loves order, makes the property owner happy because things are now neat and clean. Do you get the picture? When you do what you love, no matter what that is, you are in service to others. Do not sell yourself short! You are here for a reason. Every person has a place. Every occupation is needed to create balance. Right now, your planet is out of balance because of the hierarchical system you've created. That thought process needs to be banished. Respect needs to be given to every occupation. That creates balance. That creates pride in every individual who is executing the talents they came here to express. How joyful!

K: Wow, that is beautiful, thank you! Yes, we need to eliminate stigmas on this planet. Let everyone and encourage everyone to be who they came here to be.

R: As it exists today, Earth is a very difficult school. Souls come here to learn some very difficult lessons. If the balance between people was there, those lessons could still be learned but in a different way.

K: How do you mean? As it exists today, the unusual or the traumatic is what people tend to remember. If the balance between people existed, those lessons could still be learned but might not have the same impact as the hard lessons. For the soul to evolve, those lessons need to stick, they need to last and be part of the soul's growth and evolution. If those lessons are too easy, that might not happen. But isn't the idea enlightenment? Where everything a soul thinks, says, and does come from love?

R: True. And certain souls will and have attained that. But they were able to do that because of other souls who either were unwilling, unable, or agreed to serve as an antagonist for the evolved soul. So, a certain kind of balance already exists in your human structure. It is indeed a matrix of epic proportions.

K: I guess so! Just when I think I'm about to get this thing called life figured out, you throw a wrench into it, and I'm confused all over again.

R: That's the idea! That's why you're here. To begin to understand and pass that information on to others who are beginning to understand, too.

K: Will I ever understand?

R: When it is your turn to transition, yes, it will become clear.

K: Oh, good grief.

K: What do the people on our planet most need to know today?

R: It really is up to the individual and where they are on their soul path. However, no matter where they are, the most important thing for all people to know is that we truly are all one. We all come from source and to source we will return. Once people realize that they will begin to love themselves, love others, love and take care of their home. Where do you think Earth came from? It, like all other planets, stars, and life forms come from source, too.

K: That is so important but how do we get that message across to people?

R: Lead by example. Live your life according to the Law of One. When others are ready, they too will influence others. You can't force people to do anything. You live your life according to the Law of One, which means taking care of yourself and taking care of others. That doesn't necessarily mean taking care of everybody. Use the talents you brought with you in this life and use them to help others. By others, those others who want or need help. That doesn't include everybody. You can't teach, influence, or even rescue those who don't want to be taught, influenced, or rescued.

K: I was going to ask my next question which is what is the most important thing people need to know about the future, but I think you already answered that question along with the last question. Is that correct?

R: Yes, that is correct. All anybody needs to know ever is that we are all one. We are all a piece of divinity. Some people will say that you need to treat others like you treat yourself. More false words have never been spoken! Most people treat themselves horribly! Most people treat others far better than they treat themselves. Once people understand that we are all one, they'll understand that there is no separation. There is no you/me. There is no us/them. There is only One. It kind of pays homage to the phrase, he shot off his foot to spite his face. It makes no sense but that is how people treat others. They treat others like the foot in this scenario, to spite their face or themselves. When you break it down in simple terms, it sounds as ridiculous as it is.

On another level, however, people are on Earth to evolve; to really understand that we are all one. It can take hundreds of lifetimes to learn that lesson. Only the bravest of souls will come to Earth. Souls do understand that they will arrive with little to no memory of their life as a soul or that they are a piece of divinity. They arrive as if they are blind, deaf, and with both hands and feet tied behind their backs. Is it any wonder people sometimes act as they do? It is courageous to attempt to remember that you are a spirit. It can take not only one lifetime, but it can take many lifetimes to remember. Even when those spirits do remember, life is still not easy.

People need to have patience and understand that just because they have begun to remember, not everyone is in the same place or at the same soul age. Your job is not to judge those that are of a younger soul age than you. Your job is to lead by example, so those younger than you have a guidepost should they choose to follow it. Take those by the hand that want to be shown. Leave the others to their own choices, their own lives, and their own lessons. They too will age and take on the same responsibilities as you're taking on now. Let them evolve as they choose.

Think about it; even those souls who understand the Law of One don't always live it. Do you?

K: Ah, hmm, no, not always.

R: Just because you understand the concept, doesn't mean you've incorporated it into your way of being. You too are still learning. It's like a 6th grader teaching a 1st grader. They certainly can teach, but only to a point. They can't teach what they don't know. The same is true of the spirit world on Earth. Those who claim to be awakened really are not. They are in the process of awakening. If they knew everything, they would no longer be human. They would be back to source. So, anyone who is still in human form has not learned everything. They can begin to teach others if they choose, and if others want to learn, but they cannot teach them everything because they've not yet experienced that while in human form. That is impossible.

It is incredibly hard work to be human, but it is also a privilege. This becomes obvious when you see how many humans take their own lives. No one is judging them. There is nothing but compassion from the other side – from those that understand how difficult human life can be. Those souls that take their own life have not failed. They simply bit off more than they could chew, so to speak. They thought they could handle what life was all about. What most people don't take into consideration is that there is free will for themselves, but also for other people.

When souls make their life plans there is much room for free will with their own choices and behaviors. They have no control over other people's free will choices. That is what has not been planned for or thought about when the life plan is being finalized.

Life is usually harder than anyone anticipates because you can't control others and people then make life even harder than it already is. Many can't handle it and take their own lives, so they don't have to continue living a life they really don't want.

All know that they will have the opportunity to come back and try again and even alter that plan, so it is more compatible with what they are trying to accomplish this time around. Most people at one time in their life have suicidal thoughts. They don't tell people, because of fear of being judged or being shamed. This is just another reminder to not judge anyone else on their journey. You don't know what soul age they are, what they came here to learn, and how many other lives they've lived attempting to do what they are doing now.

September 5, 2022

K: You mentioned that you are from the planet Eurates. Is that in a particular star system?

R: Yes, it is in the Andromedin star system. Most people have heard of Andromeda but don't understand that there are planets within that star system.

K: I thought you said you lived on the rings of Saturn.

R: That is true as well. My origins are from Eurates in the Andromedin star system, but I now reside on the rings of Saturn with the other members of the Ramadear collective. Just like you were born in Sioux Falls, but now reside in Omaha. In addition, you have lived many other places in your United States. The same is true of the collective. We have origins, we have where we live now but we also have thousands of other places where we have resided.

K: OK, that now makes sense to me. Thank you.

K: When will people wake up to the fact that we are all one; that we've all experienced lives of every gender and every ethnicity?

R: Because that statement is not true. Not every human has experienced a life as a different gender or a different ethnicity. The youngest of souls have not had that experience yet which is one of the reasons racism and misogyny exist on your planet today.

K: I never quite thought of it that way. I guess I went back to the thought that everybody has had multiple lives on Earth and therefore should perhaps be a bit more enlightened.

R: For many people this is their first life on Earth. Some are highly evolved spirits so arrive with a different mindset – in other words they come in knowing we are all one. Others that are considered newer or younger souls are victims of their initial Earthly programming. The highly evolved spirits are here to raise the vibration on Earth, not necessarily evolve. They are here to help others evolve. For the younger souls, they are here to evolve and maybe have not had the opportunity yet to experience lives as another gender or race. Not to worry. They will all have hundreds of opportunities to experience these things.

K: On that note, why does racism even exist at all? What started it?

R: One of the many and varied reasons racism exists is because when a soul chooses its first Earth incarnation, it carries those experiences into the next incarnations. If they choose repeatedly to be of a certain race or gender, they might come into life not understanding anything than what they've already experienced. Confusion and fear step in and there you have the beginnings of racism. Fear is the trigger. They don't understand because they've never experienced life as another race. (Or gender)

Another reason is that programming from a previous life where one race was considered better than another race is brought into the next life. The prejudices came with the package, so to speak. Especially if they decided to incarnate into a family which already believes and expresses hate and disdain for a group of people unlike themselves. The programming of the existing family compounds with the programming of a previous life or lives.

Another reason might be to experience the life of a person who either was discriminated against or the opposite and experience life as a dominant. This takes the subject to a whole different level where Karma now comes into play. Perhaps someone was a racist in one life and has chosen to experience a life as the one who is discriminated against to atone for behavior from that past life. They want to experience what they inflicted on someone else.

If they choose to be a racist in this life, it could be because they were a racist in a past life and want to repeat the circumstances which created that behavior so they can make different choices this time around. Does it work? Sometimes yes and sometimes no. It all depends on the free will of the individual involved. This subject is so multilayered as are most reasons people decided to incarnate in human form. There is no one way, nor one answer to these questions.

Racism is a subject very much in the forefront of many societies today, as it should be. There are many souls who have chosen to incarnate in this period to right the wrongs, or at least bring to light behaviors that are not acceptable. They are very evolved souls who understand that the way to get people to change is to get them to want to change and not force change upon them. Your Martin Luther King, Jr. was a perfect example. It took his murder to really bring home his words and actions. He believed that unconditional love and unguarded truth would have the final word in reality. He began manifesting that while in human form and he continues to influence from the other side. Many are now paying attention and altering their beliefs and behaviors because of his influence. Children are now being born of mixed race. This is one of the strongest ways to eliminate racism. When one of those children is your child or grandchild you begin to see the child, not the race. That is what any society needs – to see the person not the race. To take it one step further, people need to begin to see the soul – not the person or the race or the gender. When more people begin to look deeply into the eyes which, yes, are the window to the soul, they will see a human struggling just like they are. They will see a human just trying to live a life in a world that is struggling as well.

September 6, 2022

K: Let's go back to The Law of One.

R: Yes, that is fine.

K: I'm getting a basic understanding although I am only finished book two out of five, but I do find it a bit difficult to understand. Can you help with that?

R: That is what you and I are doing with this book. I'm sending you information that can be easily understood by the modern human race. At least the modern human who has an interest and curiosity about life, spirituality, and what is beyond what they can touch, see, and feel.

K: Thank you. It feels like that is what we are doing as I recognize some of the language in the books being like the information you are giving me.

R: There are many of you who are doing the same thing; interpreting messages from the Ramadear collective, as well as other collectives communicating with humans on Earth. As The Law of One states, there is always distortion in what is being communicated and what is heard and then put in writing for others to read. There is no way distortion can't happen. That is why there are so many people being contacted right now. We feel that if we communicate with enough people on Earth that the real message will get through – it just might, and will, come from several different sources.

That is the base of what we are trying to tell you; read, study, and experience but understand that the messenger is delivering a distorted message. If any one messenger claims that they know it all or have it exactly right, run. That is the surest way to know there is more ego involved than true service to others. The best messengers are those who understand that they are coming from their own perspective, even if those messages are channeled verbally or through the written word from spirits on the other side.

What we must tell the world can't always be communicated with the languages available to humans today. Some of the words simply don't exist. We do our best to communicate in words humans can best understand, but please know that is the first step in distortion of the real message.

Everyone, including those souls who are the most open, cannot communicate perfectly. They can only communicate with words available to them and experiences available to them. When certain words don't exist, the human messenger tries to find words that will work, that most people will understand and relate to. The most dedicated and intelligent of you will get the translations communicated in the best way possible, but it is still up to the listener, the learner, the curious to hear or read properly and then put their own spin on things. Do you see? Now we have distortion again. From the collective to the messenger. Then from the messenger to the curious public. It's no wonder there is confusion. It's like a cosmic game of telephone tag.

What you are trying to communicate to others is said or written in a certain way, yet you have no control of how people interpret your words. As you know with your psychic readings – people will read into the messages you offer in a way that usually suits them and where they are in life right now. You have to trust that you are delivering the information that the person needs to hear that day. It is then up to them to interpret based on their own ideals.

K: Still, that's an immense amount of responsibility to place on the messengers.

R: Yes, that is why we are careful in whom we choose. It's not always just because you say yes. You have to say yes to receiving information and we have to say yes trusting that you will be moral, truthful, and honest with the information provided. There are many so called messengers that are coming from service to self, rather than service to others. The messages they deliver will be self-serving under the guise of service to others. Pick your teachers/messengers carefully. Read, listen, attend classes as much as you like, but be careful with what you believe. Believe only what resonates with your soul and makes your heart sing. If information doesn't feel right in your soul or if the messenger is using words to control, shame, or belittle you, that is not a true message from us or any collective.

A messenger should be truly in service to others, which means they want the same thing for you; for you to find what makes you happy, what makes your heart sing while being of service to others too.

K: That is my mission on this planet! To help people step into their own power. Many people misinterpret thinking that means they are better than others. Nothing could be further from the truth! Stepping into one's own power means to understand that they come from source as does everyone. We truly are one. When you help another out of love, you help yourself. The more you separate yourself from others through ego, the worse you will feel and the further from source you will be.

Yes, I know, you cannot be far from source when you ARE source.

R: We are glad you caught that! They can only FEEL that they are separate from source. They are as close as everyone else they just don't know it. Still, we cannot judge that. Perhaps that's what they came to Earth to learn; to feel separate. If that's the case, they are doing it beautifully. In the work you are doing, you appeal to those who feel separated but no longer want to feel that way. They want a better understanding of life, why they are here, and that they deserve to be happy. You'd be amazed to realize how many people don't want to know that information. They are content with not knowing or having power over others. They think that's what makes them happy but again, nothing could be further from the truth.

K: I've been telling people for some time now that we are all one. Sometimes the response I get is, "Why?" I tell people that God is everything and is pure love. He/she wants to experience everything that has ever been, or ever will be. That is why we split off from source/God and become separate from each other so as individual pieces of divinity we can experience everything that has ever been or ever will be. Is this correct? If so, can you elaborate? If not, can you give a better explanation? If we all are working our way back to Source/God, why do we split off from Source/God in the first place? If we are already nothing but love, why do we need to have our souls evolve? Evolve into what? To what we already are? I don't really understand.

R: This is a great question. This goes back to the knowledge that we all know who we are in spirit but choose to become human. When we arrive as humans, we have no memory of what our spirit life is like. Being human is just something we've chosen to experience. The same is true when we spilt off from Source/God. It is simply something we want to experience. Some choose to be human, some choose to be spirit guides, some choose to be extraterrestrials, some choose to be just a source of light. God is pure energy – love energy. It is with this love energy that choices are given. Think of your body. It is one whole thing, correct?

K: Yes, that is true.

R: You still can make one hand do something independent of the other or even independent of your leg or your head. It is your choice or your free will that gives you these kinds of choices, yet you are still one being. The same is true of Source/God. It is one thing, (everything) but parts can be or move or experience independent of the other parts. No matter what, everything is still a piece of the whole, a piece of divinity.

K: Thank you that's becoming a bit clearer. But then why are some spirits negative or do negative things and other spirits think and act out of love?

R: Here is a crude example: Your hand can waive. Your hand can also show a middle finger to someone in an act of hate, frustration, or anger. It's the same hand but doing different things with a very different intent.

K: Well, you're right. That was a pretty crude example, but certainly got the point across.

R: The same is true of Source/God. What is still considered Source/God can show positive and negative energy. Remember, there is no light without darkness. For every "thing" there is an opposing force. It is part of the experience of Source/God. So, in some ways you are correct. Source/God is experiencing everything that has ever been or ever will be. That is the essence of love. Free will, choices, for all.

When you answer the question of why, please continue answering the way you have been but add the caveat that everyone creates their own reality. Maybe this isn't what Source/God really is or wants. Maybe everyone is making it all up.

K: Are they? Are they making it all up?

R: Are you? Are you making all this up?

K: I don't know. Am I?

R: You are certainly creating your life as you know it, but then so is everybody else. It just feels real. When you leave your human body, you will have a better understanding. You will not yet understand it all, but you will certainly have a better understanding.

K: Why won't we understand it all when we leave our human bodies?

R: Here is an analogy – think of the ocean as source. If you take a bucket of water out of the ocean, it is still ocean water, correct? Now take a teaspoon out of the bucket of water. It is still ocean water, correct?

Now think of this ocean scenario - If that teaspoon of ocean water goes back into the bucket of ocean water and then goes back to the whole of the ocean water does it understand that it is and always was the ocean?

K: I would think so, yes.

R: You are correct. But does that blended teaspoon and bucket of ocean water understand what it's like in the far reaches of the ocean?

K: I don't know. Does it?

R: Not until it has been poured back into the main source of the ocean. In other words, until it has experienced every part of every ocean. This is very similar to what you are experiencing as a human, as a spirit, as a soul, as a guide, as an extraterrestrial. You won't understand it all until you've experienced it all.

K: I'm beginning to understand! When will I experience it all? When will I be done?

R: You missed the point. You will never experience it all. You will never be done. You have the mistaken notion that when you leave your human body that you will be done. This is not true. You will be done experiencing one small piece of the expansion. How long will it take that teaspoon of water to experience every part of every ocean? The example I've just used is a very small scale compared to Source/God and its vastness. It is never ending. It is infinite. So, you see, you will never be done! You might be done being human eventually, but you will never be done experiencing what your piece of soul broke off to experience. You are energy. Energy never dies, it only changes form. Are you getting a better understanding of what that really means?

K: I think so. What I've found is that so many people think just in human terms. They keep everything separate. In a way, we are separate as bits of energy. But that energy is so much more than human or the soul that exists when we exit the human body.

R: Exactly! Now you're beginning to understand that you will never understand! How's that for the big cosmic joke?

K: Pretty darn good, I'd say.

September 9, 2022

K: How can people find more joy in their lives?

R: People can find more joy when they realize that being human is real only in the sense of what they want to learn and how they can grow. It is more of an illusion than anything. Everyone is here for the same reason – to be of service to others – yet they are all here for a different reason – to express that service to others in their own unique way.

When people realize these two vital things, they will be taking the first step to happiness. When people realize we are all the same yet uniquely different, they can be happy finding what makes them happy without worrying about what anyone else thinks. You see it doesn't matter what anyone else thinks because it will be guaranteed to be different! They have to trust that they are doing "it" correctly, even if there is no one else around to validate or approve. When you are truly connected with your guides and angels, they will give you the validation you are seeking.

K: What validation is that?

R: You will find yourself being happy! What you are seeking is already with you. It is up to you to "unzip" yourselves, dig deep and find it. Happiness is not outside of yourself. Happiness is within. It always has been and always will be. Go claim it – claim your happy life.

K: You make it sound so easy.

R: It really is when you boil it down. People make things too hard. Life is hard enough without people adding to it. Focus for a minute on the people around you. Have you noticed that when things are great and going your way friends and family will congratulate you and then move on to another subject? Sometimes they don't even congratulate you! They try to keep you "in your place." But when you are having a bad day, week, month, or even year, people want to hear all about it. They don't necessarily want to do anything about it, but they do want all the juicy details. Mostly so they can then share their troubles with you – how they can relate to you. It is really a backward way of connecting with people. Next time someone you know achieves something which they are proud of, congratulate them! Ask for all the details of how they accomplished what they accomplished. Pay rapt attention.

When someone is having a bad day/week/month/year ask them how you can be of help. Listen, help if asked, empathize with them, but don't reward victimhood. Everyone has bad times in their life, and they deserve friendship and assistance. What they don't need is the kind of attention which rewards negative thinking. Even people having a bad time of it, but who are ultimately positive people, will feel the pain and very soon begin to pull themselves out of this bad place and bring themselves to a place of richer rewards – happiness. Those who have a bad time for simply attention will only want more of the same. Their reward is the attention they crave, and they've found it through being a victim. Lather, rinse, repeat. Yes, be there for your fellow man to help lift them when they need it. Believe us, we all need it from time to time. Just don't hand out sympathy rewards for staying stuck. Help don't enable.

September 27, 2022

K: Over the past weeks I've overheard some interesting comments that I'd like you to clarify or explain.

R: Go ahead

K: I heard that junk DNA is actually where God resides in us all. Is that true?

R: Yes and no. Yes, it is true that the DNA that is yet only identified as junk DNA does hold the energy of God. The no part is that God resides in every part of you – not just your DNA or junk DNA.

K: I just think using the term junk DNA sounds so unenlightened and dismissive.

R: It is only labeled that until it is scientifically identified.

K: Will that happen in my lifetime? Or ever?

R: Yes, scientists are currently getting very close to identifying a section of junk DNA. They are just confused as to what they are actually seeing. Part of it is alien in origin so they have nothing to compare it to. It is also different for each individual. That's part of why they are confused; what they're seeing is different in specific individuals. They have yet to find consistency. Until they do that, the studies will continue. Scientists need to prove and prove again to present things to the public. They are as yet unable to do that.

What they might come forward with is that they are making progress with identifying junk DNA but have discovered things from unknown origins. They'll begin speaking about it but leave it vague and open to speculation.

K: Interesting. Is that how scientists reveal other things?

R: No, not usually. Many things are discovered by accident. As we've talked about before, everything already exists. It is up to minds trained in a particular field to claim and capture what already exists and bring it to public consciousness. When it comes to certain discoveries scientists are very careful to reveal what they know due to controversy, judgement, and the possible destruction of careers they've worked hard to build. Certain controversial things have been discovered and squashed by corporations and politicians because of the repercussions to the profits of various organizations. These discoveries are stuck in a vault somewhere where they are not available, not only to the public but to the scientific community as well.

K: Well, that's a little scary, not to mention unfair.

R: Follow the money – always follow the money. Money is the God of your culture so indeed it does reside in junk DNA of individuals.

K: Here's another comment I overheard. Do for God to be loved. Wow, that seems a bit threatening to me. What is your explanation?

R: Again, this is a yes and no answer.

K: Really? That's surprising. Please explain.

R: There is one word which doesn't fit. It is the word to. It should read do for God and be loved.

K: How is that any different?

R: The difference is that you cannot not do for God because you are God. So, if you do for God, you will always be loved which means regardless, you will always be loved because you are always doing for God. You have no choice because all is for God. It is humanity which judges what is and what is not for God. The truth is that ALL is for God.

When your statement reads do for God TO be loved that indicates that there is the option to not be loved. That is the untruth. No matter what words are chosen or spoken, you are always doing for God, and you will always be loved. There is no other way.

K: Thank you. When you put it that way it makes it much clearer. The original way just had a creepy and threatening way to it.

R: How do you think humans have maintained control over others since the beginning of life on Earth? Yes, by threatening, judging, or shaming. You are in a huge expression of that currently on your planet. Once you begin to understand that all is for God and you will always be loved, the need to be "top dog" or in control of others will cease to exist. Right now, the strongest emotion for your people is that of fear. Once people are no longer afraid, they will understand that they are and will always be loved. Love is the true emotion – the only one that matters. Even the people who are beginning to understand and believe that love is the way are having a hard time living their lives that way.

They can be misunderstood, judged, ridiculed, etc. It makes it more of a challenge to come from love and express only love. That is why they are on Earth at this time; to be trailblazers and to learn how to still come from love when triggered by emotions other than love. How to maintain love against all odds.

K: Here is a random question: Many years ago, I had a life review where I met my council of elders and was shown my life in holographic images of where my thoughts affected people first in a negative way and then, thank goodness, in a positive way.

Why was I given that experience and at that particular time?

R: We were concerned that you were veering off your chosen path. You were getting caught up in the corporate energy and not accelerating the way we or you intended. You were showing some level of success in the corporate world and hadn't yet made the commitment to the greater good. Your council of elders decided an intervention was necessary. Even though that intervention shook you and made a definite impact, you still weren't ready to commit to a life of service to others. It took a literal brick to fall on your head!

K: Oh yes, how could I forget that? I knew that was someone on the other side, I just didn't know who. Who was it?

R: It was one of your guides. They wish to stay anonymous as to which guide of yours. It did the trick though, didn't it?

K: I guess so! I was innocently loading my car with art supplies to go teach a class when I felt "someone" push me from behind. I told people I tripped but I know I was pushed.

R: Yes, you were certainly pushed. Your guides, as well as the collective, have been subtly trying to push you for years and you just weren't listening. You were always making progress, but that progress was at a turtle's pace.

K: I just had no faith in myself that I could make a difference or make a living in the metaphysical world. Then the not-so-subtle push came. Thirty-seven stiches in my head later, evidently was the wakeup call I needed. My art business sold, and I went public as a psychic medium. All this happened in the space of less than a year. Thirty-five years of crawling on the spiritual path and then in one year, all heaven broke loose!

R: And aren't you glad it did?

K: Of course. In many ways I wished you would have pushed me sooner.

R: You simply weren't ready earlier. The timing was actually perfect.

K: As always.

November 22, 2022

 K: As we close this book are there any final words of hope for humanity?

R: Of course. There is always hope for humanity. Remember everything always begins inside of yourself. As you all grow and evolve, you'll figure out that you are perfect, humanity is perfect, the matrix of life is perfect. You will finally accept self-love. When you learn to love yourselves, loving everyone else is easy. When you finally grasp what life is all about, then loving yourself and loving others is the most natural thing that exists….because love IS the only thing that exists.

God wouldn't have allowed Earth and the Earth lessons to exist if there wasn't hope for humanity. It's like watching a toddler learn to walk. First, they learn to crawl. Then they pull themselves up onto furniture. Next, they learn to walk. Some children do this in a relatively short span of time. Other children take longer. Is one child wrong and the other right? No. children, as with everyone, will learn; they just learn at their own rate. When a child is born, do the parents wonder if their child will ever walk? No, they trust, they assume, they know that the child will eventually walk. (Of course, there are exceptions with children of special needs.)

The same is true with humanity. We have faith that humans will eventually crawl, pull themselves up and eventually walk. It is the way of things. It is the way it should be. It is the way it is. Some of you haven't even learned to crawl yet. Others are crawling, others are pulling themselves up, and still others are walking – all at different times and at different rates. The faith and the expectation are there that humanity in all its forms will walk and even run. It is the path to love.

And So It Is.

Desiderata

Go placidly amid the noise and haste,

And remember what peace there may be in silence.

As far as possible without surrender

Be on good terms with all persons.

Speak your truth quietly and clearly;

And listen to others,

Even the dull and ignorant;

They too have their story.

Avoid loud and aggressive persons,

They are vexations to the spirit.

If you compare yourself with others,

You may become vain and bitter;

For always there will be greater and lesser persons than yourself.

Enjoy your achievements as well as your plans.

Keep interested in your career, however humble;

It is a real possession in the changing fortunes of time.

Exercise caution in your business affairs;

For the world is full of trickery.

But let this not blind you to what virtue there is;

Many persons strive for high ideals;

And everywhere life is full of heroism.

Be yourself.

Especially do not feign affection.

Neither be cynical about love;

For in the face or all aridity and disenchantment

It is perennial as the grass.

Take kindly the council of the years,

Gracefully surrendering the things of youth.

Nurture strength of spirit to shield you in sudden misfortune.

But do not distress yourself with dark imaginings.

Many fears are born of fatigue and loneliness.

Beyond a wholesome discipline,

Be gently with yourself.

You are a child of the universe,

No less than the trees and stars;

You have a right to be here.

And whether or not it is clear to you,

No doubt the universe is unfolding as it should.

Therefore be at peace with God,

Whatever you conceive Him to be,

And whatever your labors and aspirations,

In the noisy confusion of life, keep peace with your soul.

With all its sham, drudgery, and broken dreams,

It is still a beautiful world.

Be cheerful.

Strive to be happy.

Max Ehrmann

Acknowledgements

There are always so many people to thank when sending a book out to the universe. First, and most important, I'd like to thank God, Creator, Source. I've finally realized that what I was taught as a child couldn't be further from the truth. I always questioned that if God is all loving, then why should we fear him? I never got a reasonable answer until I began my own spiritual path. God IS all loving. Period. End of sentence. Fear is the opposite of God.

Next, I want to thank Ramadear and the Ramadear collective. Their insistence that I keep writing this book even during times I became disenchanted. Their ability to communicate through me with words to humanity is completely humbling. I hope I didn't disappoint them.

Thank you to Roxanne Wach for her talents and ability to make whatever I send her not only pretty but within the guidelines and requirements to publish.

Thank you to my darling friend, Marina Gray, who took the picture you see on the cover. We were on vacation together in northern California when Ramadear spoke to me telling me to put down my journal and enjoy my friend.

Thank you to the metaphysical community locally, nationally, and globally. I learn from you wise souls every day and add your wisdom to my toolbox of spiritual magic.

Thank you to my spirit guides who, thank goodness, have a great sense of humor when I accuse them of drinking on the job. Their patience is never ending. I expect that when I transition back to spirit, they will hit the bar for the next millennia and pray I choose to never incarnate as a human again.

About the Author

Kristi Pederson is a psychic medium, author, and speaker who lives in Omaha, NE. Her mission in this life is to help others stand in their own power and understand their own greatness.

Her other books are **An Extraordinary Life**, published in 2010, **We Are Not Alone: My Extraterrestrial Contact**, published in 2019, and **Between Earth and Heaven...a beginners guide to living a spiritual life**, published in 2021.

The documentary, *We Are Not Alone*, produced, filmed, and edited by Illuminating Hearts and Tiny Space Productions, was released January 2023, and is based on her book, *We Are Not Alone: My Extraterrestrial Contact*.